T0327048

EROTIC POEMS FROM THE SANSKRIT

Translations from the Asian Classics

TRANSLATIONS FROM THE ASIAN CLASSICS

Editorial Board

Wm. Theodore de Bary, Chair

Paul Anderer

Donald Keene

George A. Saliba

Haruo Shirane

Burton Watson

Wei Shang

Erotic Poems from the Sanskrit

An Anthology

Edited and translated by
R. PARTHASARATHY

Columbia University Press | New York

Columbia University Press wishes to express its appreciation for assistance given by the Pushkin Fund in the publication of this book.

Columbia University Press
Publishers Since 1893
New York Chichester, West Sussex
cup.columbia.edu
Copyright © 2017 Columbia University Press
All rights reserved
Library of Congress Cataloging-in-Publication Data
Names: Parthasarathy, R., 1934- editor, translator.
Title: Erotic poems from the Sanskrit : an anthology / [edited and translated by] R. Parthasarathy.
Description: New York : Columbia University Press, 2017. | Series: Translations from the Asian classics | Includes bibliographical references nd index.
Identifiers: LCCN 2016059358 (print) | LCCN 2017019170 (ebook) | ISBN 9780231545464 (electronic) | ISBN 9780231184380 (cloth : acid-free paper) | ISBN 9780231184397 (pbk. : acid-free paper)
Subjects: LCSH: Erotic poetry, Sanskrit—Translations into English. | Sanskrit poetry—Translations into English.
Classification: LCC PK4474.A3 (ebook) | LCC PK4474.A3 E76 2017 (print) | DDC 891/.2100803538—dc23
LC record available at https://lccn.loc.gov/2016059358

Columbia University Press books are printed on permanent and durable acid-free paper.

Printed in the United States of America
Cover design: Jordan Wannemacher
Cover illustration: *Rādhā*, Rajasthani, Kishangarh, ca. 1740–1748; courtesy of the National Museum, New Delhi; © photo alamy.com

For

Mohan

Arjun

Gautam and Masako

CONTENTS

ACKNOWLEDGMENTS

I thank Terence Diggory, Barry Goldensohn, Robert Goodwin, and Christopher McVey for their comments on early drafts of the manuscript. I am indebted to David Shulman for his insightful remarks on eight of the poems. I have benefited from the suggestions of the two anonymous reviewers, which helped to improve the manuscript immeasurably. My thanks are due to Amy Syrell and Marilyn Sheffer of the Interlibrary Loan Service of the Lucy Scribner Library at Skidmore College for getting me the Sanskrit books I needed. My greatest debt is to my wife, Shobhan, who read and reread the manuscript carefully several times. If the poems speak to us, it is in large measure because of her keen ear and good sense.

Jennifer Crewe, associate provost and director, Columbia University Press, was from the beginning enthusiastic about the work. Her encouragement and patience were exemplary during my final revisions of the manuscript. My editor, Jonathan Fiedler, and Leslie Kriesel, assistant managing editor, were unfailing in their support. To Mike Ashby, my copyeditor, I am indebted for his meticulous editing of the manuscript. He saw to every detail, and nothing seemed to escape his watchful eye.

Grateful acknowledgment is made to the editors of the following magazines in which some of these poems first appeared, either in earlier or current versions:

Indian Literature: "The Bed," "The Lamp," "The Pledge," "Wild Nights"
Manushi: "Bitter Harvest," "The Riverbank"

Modern Poetry in Translation: "Aubade," "The Red Seal," "The Traveler," "A Word of Advice"
Poetry (Chicago): "The Sheets"
Verse: "Jewels," "Then and Now," "Who Needs the Gods?"
Weber Studies: "The Art of Poetry," "Complaint"

INTRODUCTION

This selection of poems is personal; it does not attempt to be representative of Sanskrit poetry in general. It comprises poems that I have enjoyed reading and that have excited me. I have also selected them because I found these poems manageable within the resources of modern English verse. The selection is intended for the general reader and lovers of poetry who might want to know what Sanskrit poetry is like. It offers a salutary corrective to the notion, still prevalent in the West, that Indians in the past were predominantly otherworldly and spiritually minded. Nothing could be further from the truth. These poems reflect a culture that celebrates the pleasures of the flesh without any inhibition in a language that never gives offense, that never crosses the line but always observes the canons of good taste. In this the Sanskrit poets are our contemporaries despite the centuries that separate us. The poems speak simply and passionately to a wide range of human experience—love fulfilled and love unfulfilled, old age, poverty, asceticism, and nature—in a voice that moves us even today.

The introduction makes no pretense to scholarship; it attempts to provide some basic information to the reader who comes to Sanskrit poetry for the first time and who needs guidance on how to read a Sanskrit poem in translation. The notes at the back of the book throw light on specific elements of the poems such as language, imagery, and tone as well as on culture-specific references. My goal is a modest one: to awaken the interest of the reader in the poem by providing him or her with such tools as are necessary for the enterprise. Wherever possible, the poems are read in a comparative context, with examples from Greek, Latin, English, Chinese, Tamil, and Prākrit poetry.

Erotic Poems from the Sanskrit comprises poems by seventy-two poets, including seven women poets and thirty-five anonymous poets, from sixteen works composed, with two exceptions, between the fourth and seventeenth centuries. The poets are presented alphabetically for the convenience of the reader.

For a long time, three anthologies of Sanskrit poetry in English translation have held the field: Ingalls (1965),[1] Brough (1968),[2] and Merwin and Masson (1977).[3] These anthologies have contributed significantly to our understanding and enjoyment of Sanskrit poetry. Since then, other translations of Sanskrit poetry have appeared and enriched the field: Miller (1978),[4] Selby (2000),[5] and Bailey and Gombrich (2005).[6] *Erotic Poems from the Sanskrit* builds upon the work of these distinguished translators. It offers a new verse translation that introduces the richness and variety of Sanskrit poetry to a new generation of readers in a robust, contemporary English idiom that captures, insofar as possible, the tone and register of the Sanskrit originals. The translations are, above all, English poems that can be read with pleasure by readers of poetry.

Love in all its aspects is a favorite theme of the Sanskrit poets. Poems on the topic of erotic love (*kāma*) form the centerpiece of the anthologies, and the translations reflect this preference. The poems are often sexually explicit but they never offend our taste. In their openness to the sexual experience, they have a contemporary flavor to them. Readers who wish to have a greater understanding of Sanskrit erotic poetry might want to familiarize themselves with the conventions of the erotic mood spelled out in such texts as Vātsyāyana's *Kāmasūtra* (The book of love, 4th cent.) or Kalyāṇamalla's *Anaṅgaraṅga* (The stage of the Bodiless One, 16th cent.). Sanskrit erotic poetry has few equals, with the possible exception of the erotic poems in the so-called Greek Anthology, compiled by the Byzantine scholar Constantinus Cephalas in the tenth century in Constantinople.

Translation from one language into another involves some loss, as the Buddhist monk and prolific translator Kumārajīva (344–413) famously reminded us: "In the process of translating a Sanskrit text into Chinese it loses all its nuances. . . . It's something like chewing cooked rice and then feeding it to another person. Not only has it lost its flavor; it will also make him want to throw up."[7] Despite the eminent monk's opinion, it is possible to carry across the *flavor* of a poem from one language to another. And that is precisely what this selection has attempted to do.

Among the problems I wrestled with in making these translations, the hardest one perhaps was how to make the Sanskrit poems heard in English. Here tone and register are crucial factors. English does not have a tradition of erotic poetry comparable to that of Sanskrit. The sexual explicitness of some of the poems may not be to the taste of some readers. As a result, I had to modify the tone and register without compromising the integrity of the poems. In translating from Sanskrit into English, one translates not just the text but also an entire culture and worldview that remain hidden like so many roots beneath the text.

THE ROLE OF THE POET

What precisely was the role of the poet in the Indian tradition? In the Rig Veda (ca. 1200–900 B.C.E.) we are told,

> Varuṇa confided in me, the wise one:
> Thrice seven names has the cow. Who knows the trail
> should whisper them like secrets, if he is to speak
> to future generations as an inspired poet.[8]

According to the commentator Sāyaṇa (14th cent.), speech (*vāc*) in the form of a cow (*aghnya*) has twenty-one meters corresponding to her breast, throat, and head. Only after the intervention of Varuṇa (Vedic god of natural and moral law) does the poet who is the wise one (*medhira*) become the inspired one (*vipra*). His exceptional knowledge imposes a responsibility on him. He is both the keeper and the transmitter of the tradition that regarded poetry as a way of knowledge. It was believed that the spoken word, properly formulated, could produce a physical effect on the world. The word was invested with sacred power. This image of the poet as a seer (*ṛṣi*) in the Vedic period gives way in later times to that of the poet as a learned man of refined sensibility and taste (*kavi*) who made his living as a court poet. Not all poets were, however, fortunate enough to make their living as court poets. The case of the Kashmiri poet Bilhaṇa (11th cent.) comes to mind. After many unsuccessful attempts to find a patron, he eventually found one in the Cāḷukya king Vikramāditya VI Tribhuvanamalla (r. 1076–1126) of Kalyāṇa (present-day Basavakalyan in Bidar District, Karnataka). He repaid his patron a hundredfold by composing a fulsome panegyric in his honor, *The Deeds of His Majesty Vikramāṅka* (*Vikramāṅkadevacarita*).

The twelfth-century poet and critic Kṣemendra, also from Kashmir, takes an exalted view of the poet's vocation.

> A poet should learn with his eyes
> the forms of leaves
> he should know how to make
> people laugh when they are together
> he should get to see
> what they are really like
> he should know about oceans and mountains
> in themselves
> and the sun and the moon and the stars
> his mind should enter into the seasons
> he should go
> among many people
> in many places
> and learn their languages.[9]

Works on poetics, such as Rājaśekhara's (10th cent.) *An Inquiry into Poetry* (*Kāvyamīmāṃsa*), offer elaborate accounts of a poet's education and of the faculties he must possess in order to be a poet.[10] His readers and listeners would, like him, be connoisseurs (*sahṛdayas*) and would be educated and endowed with similar faculties. Poetry was a highly cultivated art. It was patronized by kings and flourished in their courts. A. Berriedale Keith has described the situation well: "The great poets of India wrote for audiences of experts; they were masters of the learning of their day, long trained in the use of language, and they aimed to please by subtlety, not simplicity of effect. They had at their disposal a singularly beautiful speech, and they commanded elaborate and most effective metres."[11]

Sanskrit literary culture has been the subject of research and study in recent years.[12] I have provided, wherever necessary, historical contexts for the poets: the circumstances and constraints under which they wrote, the sort of reception their work received, and the frustrations they experienced in their search for a patron. Sanskrit was an "artificial" language learned after a "natural" language (Prākrit) had been learned. It was restricted to the educated classes and was used in the courts and in religious institutions. As a pan-Indian language, it was not tied to any specific region. As a result, Sanskrit poetry came to have a pan-Indian audience. The court was the epicenter of Sanskrit literary culture. It included poets, scholars, professional reciters of poetry, and storytellers. At poets' gatherings organized by the court, poems were recited or sung; poetry was not meant to be read. Poets flocked to the court in search of patronage; in return, they sang the praises of the king.

The Sanskrit poet rarely expresses his own thoughts and feelings. The notion of individual self-expression was foreign to the culture at that time. What the poet expresses are the thoughts and feelings of the personae in a given situation: the unfaithful husband returning home at dawn after a night with a courtesan, the wife overjoyed on seeing her husband return from his travels abroad, the hermit expressing his disaffection with the world, and so on. The poet's originality lies in the way he exploits words, images, and meter, in fact all the resources of the language, to make an expertly crafted poem that would redound to his glory.

READING A SANSKRIT POEM

The introduction offers close readings of a number poems in the light of Sanskrit poetics. Let us look at an anonymous poem, "The Sheets" (p. 15), from *Amaru's One Hundred Poems* (*Amaruśataka*, 7th cent.), an influential anthology of erotic verse, transcribed in roman type, followed by a word-for-word translation and a verse translation. The original poems do not have titles. I have provided the titles for the translations.

kvacittāṃbūlāktaḥ kvacidagarupaṅkāṅkamalinaḥ
  kvaciccūrṇodgārī kvaccidapi ca sālaktakapadaḥ |
valībhaṅgābhogairalakapatitaiḥ sīrṇakusumaiḥ
  striyā nānāvasthaṃ prathayati ratam pracchadapaṭaḥ ||

/here-[with] betel juice-smudged/[1] /here-[with]
  aloe-paste-burnished/[2]
/here-powder-rising/[3] /here-even and painted [with]
  lac-footprints/[4]
/folds-crumpled-winding-hair-fallen strewn-flowers/[5]
/[the] woman's [in] every-position celebrate pleasure-of-making-
  love [the] sheets/[6]

The virgules indicate phrase or clause boundaries that are marked with Arabic numerals.

Smudged here with betel juice, burnished there
with aloe paste, a splash of powder in one corner,
and lac from footprints painted in another,
with flowers from her hair strewn all over
its winding crumpled folds, the sheets celebrate
the woman's pleasure of making love in every position.[13]

The verse form is a single stanza of four lines (*muktaka*), the commonest of all forms in Sanskrit poetry. The stanza, and not the line as in Greek and Latin poetry, is the basic structural unit. The first three lines of the poem comprise noun (e.g., *agaru paṅkāṅka*, "aloe paste") and verb (e.g., *kvacit aktaḥ*, "smudged here") phrases; they lack the subject-predicate structure of a clause. The subject (*pracchadapaṭaḥ*, "the sheets") and the verb (*prathayati*, "celebrate") appear only in line 4. The inflectional nature of the language allows this freedom. The entire stanza is one sentence.

The word "sheets" has long been part of the euphemisms for lovemaking. Expressions include "between the sheets," "possess a woman's sheets," and "shaking of the sheets." Social conventions, however, prohibit the poet from describing the various positions. He gets around the prohibition by describing the traces left by the woman, who was probably a courtesan (*gaṇikā*), on the bedsheets during lovemaking. The telltale marks on the sheets—"betel juice," "aloe paste," "splash of powder," "lac from footprints," and "flowers from her hair"—bear witness to a night of wild lovemaking by the woman.

By concentrating almost entirely on the background, the poet forces the reader's attention on the foreground—the woman's lovemaking in "every position." In his *Interpretation of Love* (*Śṛṅgāradīpikā*, ca. 1400), one of the four commentaries on *Amaru's One Hundred Poems*, the commentator Vemabhūpāla identifies each of the telltale marks with a specific position: the "betel juice" with the "position of the cat"; the "aloe paste" with the "position of the elephant"; the "splash of powder" with the "position of the cow"; and "lac from footprints" with the unorthodox position, the woman on top of the man.[14] Vātsyāyana's *Kāmasūtra* offers the classic description of these positions (2.6 and 8).[15]

Sanskrit poetry is best understood in the light of two key concepts: *rasa* and *dhvani*. The word *rasa* means "flavor," "relish," or "taste." "Mood" would be a better translation. Different emotions (*bhāvas*), such as passion, grief, peace, and so on, that are inherent in every human being, induce the corresponding moods (*rasas*), such as the erotic, the tragic, the peaceful, and so forth, through the power of suggestion, known as *dhvani*. The word *dhvani* means "sound," "overtones," or "resonance." "Suggestion" would be a better translation. When an image, action, or situation (stimulant, or *vibhāva*) is objectively presented in a poem, it evokes a specific emotion in the reader. Once the emotion is purged of its impurities, it calls forth the corresponding mood realized through the power of suggestion. The aesthetic experience is the outcome or culmination of the refinement of the emotion. The process implies the "elevation of the consciousness of the poet and the reader from the plane of their private everyday world to the plane of collective human experience where poetry is created and enjoyed."[16] Each poem will have a dominant *rasa*, and the means of achieving it is through suggestion.

Nine *rasas* are generally recognized: the erotic, the comic, the tragic, the cruel, the heroic, the fearsome, the loathsome, the marvelous, and the peaceful. Here is a list of the stable emotions (*sthāyibhāvas*) with their corresponding moods (*rasas*).

STABLE EMOTIONS (*Sthāyibhāvas*)	MOODS (*Rasas*)
Desire (*rati*)	The erotic (*śṛṅgāra*)
Laughter (*hāsa*)	The comic (*hāsya*)
Grief (*śoka*)	The tragic (*karuṇa*)
Anger (*krodha*)	The cruel (*raudra*)
Energy (*utsāha*)	The heroic (*vīra*)
Fear (*bhaya*)	The fearsome (*bhayānaka*)
Disgust (*jugupsā*)	The loathsome (*bībhatsa*)
Wonder (*vismaya*)	The marvelous (*adbhuta*)
Peace (*śānti*)	The peaceful (*śānta*)

In the poem "The Sheets," the telltale marks on the bedsheets—"betel juice," "aloe paste," "splash of powder," "lac from footprints," and "flowers from her hair"—are images that evoke the stable emotion of desire in the reader. Purged of its impurities, desire, through the power of suggestion, culminates in the mood of erotic love, more specifically "consummation of love" (*saṃbhoga-śṛṅgāra*), an aspect of erotic love; the other being "separation in love" (*vipralamba-śṛṅgāra*). The telltale marks on the sheets suggest as much. They are the only clues the reader is offered. Familiarity with ancient Indian erotic practices will help the reader to make sense of the poem. Through the use of suggestion, the poet brings out the implicit meanings of "sheets," an image that resonates in the poem to create the mood of love in the reader.

"Sheets" is not only a tactile image but a visual and olfactory one as well. The poem is a feast of olfactory delights. It recognizes the erotic possibilities of scents such as aromatic herbs and perfumes in lovemaking. Other cultures are equally explicit on this matter. Proverbs 7:17–18 says, "I have perfumed my bed with myrrh, aloes, and cinnamon. Come, let us take our fill of love until the morning; let us solace ourselves with loves."[17]

Kalyāṇamalla's *Anaṅgaraṅga* speaks of the importance of a fine environment for lovemaking:

> Choose a courtyard that is high up in the mansion,
> that is spacious, pleasant, and newly whitewashed,
> that is perfumed by incense from aloe and other fragrant
> substances,
> that is filled with the sound of musical instruments and is bright
> with lamplight.
> Here let the man make love to the woman freely to his heart's
> content.[18]

The sense of total abandon with which the woman made love all over the bed is brought home in "The Sheets" by the insistent repetition of the adverb "here" (*kvacit*). The entire poem is one sentence wherein the subject, "the sheets" (*pracchadapaṭaḥ*), is deliberately withheld until the very end to create suspense. The poet invites the reader to experience the joy of lovemaking vicariously from behind the veil of language. The poem is an erotic masterpiece.

In the translation, the four lines of Sanskrit, each of which has seventeen syllables, have expanded to six lines in English that vary in length from nine to thirteen syllables. The classical meter is replaced by free verse. This is no doubt an impoverishment, but it is almost impossible to reproduce the quantitative meters of Sanskrit in a stress-timed language such as English. The erotic mood of the original has, I believe, come through and so has its delicate tone. The voice of the Sanskrit poet is heard distinctly. The poem's rhythmic flow is unmistakable and so is its uninhibited celebration of erotic love.

By using as few words as possible, the stanza poem achieves an unusual intensity of vision. In this union of experience and the word, the poem takes the shape of an epigram. The stanza poem remains an enduring form in Indian literature.

Culture determines a society's attitude toward sex. This perhaps explains why the Indian view of love differed from, say, the Greek view. Greek culture favored homoerotic love over heterosexual love as is evident from even a casual reading of Greek erotic poetry. If women figured in the poetic discourse, they were invariably courtesans. Take, for example, Asclepiades's "The Waistband of Hermione" (pp. xxv–xxvi) and Dioscorides's "Doris" (p. xxix). Greek women were protected from men outside their immediate family. Love poetry addressed to one's wife is nonexistent. Sanskrit erotic poetry was also composed primarily by men; as such it reflects the attitudes toward women that were common to patriarchal societies. Women who figured in Sanskrit erotic poetry were generally, but not exclusively, courtesans. Unlike Greek poetry, Sanskrit poetry offers examples of love poems about one's spouse. See, for example, "Aubade" (p. 17) and Śīlābhaṭṭārikā's "Then and Now" (p. 86).

Again, Hermione and Doris are courtesans who are mentioned by name in the poems. In Sanskrit poetry, not a single woman is mentioned by name. Women remain anonymous. The individual is replaced by the type.

Courtesans figure prominently in Sanskrit erotic poetry. The *Kāmasūtra* (6.5.28–31, 39) makes a distinction between courtesans (*gaṇikās*) and prostitutes (*veśyās*). Courtesans are highly cultivated women who are skilled in the arts and cater to a select clientele. Prostitutes, on the other hand, do not possess the exceptional qualities of the former, and they offer their services in exchange for money.

ASPECTS OF LOVE

Erotic love has two aspects: consummation of love and separation in love. The first is about lovers' meetings, both licit and illicit, and has as its object the consummation of love. The second is about lovers' partings, the breakup of relationships because the man has been unfaithful. Separations are generally only temporary; the woman forgives her philandering lover, and the two are reunited. The poems do not always specify whether the lovers are married or not.

Let us look at some poems that illustrate both aspects of love. Here is a poem, "Complaint" (p. 95), by Vidyā (fl. 7th–9th cent.), the preeminent woman poet in Sanskrit, from Vidyākara's *A Treasury of Well-Turned Verse*

(*Subhāṣitaratnakoṣa*, ca. 1100). Vidyā is comparable to Sappho (fl. ca. 600 B.C.E.) in Greek and Sulpicia (1st cent. B.C.E.) in Latin.

How fortunate you are, my friends!
You can speak openly about the goings-on
with your lovers: the idle talk, the laughter
and fun, the endless rounds of pleasure.
As for me, once my lover undid the knot of my skirt,
I swear, I remember nothing.[19]

The Sanskrit poet recognized the primacy of sight and touch in sexual relations. Vidyā offers sufficient physical details without being offensive. The detail "once my lover undid the knot of my skirt" is powerful visually and tactilely. The speaker is reluctant to talk about her experience in the presence of her friends. Orgasm renders her speechless. The experience itself is so complete that it leaves no trace of memory. Silence is the only language of intimacy. Through silence the persona indicates her unwillingness to communicate. For it is speech that binds her to the world; in silence she returns to freedom.

Sexually explicit descriptions are, generally, not common in Sanskrit poetry as they might offend against canons of good taste. Under the circumstances, when a woman is pressed for details of her lovemaking by her friends, she pretends not to remember anything of what happened. Thus her friends, together with the reader, are kept on edge by the woman's pretense. Amnesia may have been a writing convention used to overcome the social taboo against talking openly about sex. By effectively using amnesia as a trope, the poet has subverted the convention and transformed a limitation into a triumph. See also "Wild Nights" (p. 25) and Vikaṭanitambā's "The Bed" (p. 97).

The motif of untying the knot of a woman's skirt occurs elsewhere, too, as in "The Waistband of Hermione" by the Greek poet Asclepiades of Samos (4th cent. B.C.E.).

   Chance one day found us alone together
and, as happens, with one thing leading to another,

I found my fingers undoing the knot
that fastened the ceinture around her waist. It was shot
through with lime green, jet, and organdy threads,
and in tiny white lettering on the underside
these words were stitched: "Enjoy me as you wish,
though at your own peril, for other men have handled *this*."[20]

What is remarkable about the poems of Vidyā and Asclepiades is their success in breathing life into a traditional symbol such as the knot. Knots represent complications and entanglements that must be overcome before the lovers can be united. The Upaniṣads speak of untying the heart's knot to attain immortality. The Buddha (463–383 B.C.E.) taught his disciples that untying the knots of existence was the first step toward liberation (*mokṣa*) from the cycle of birth, death, and rebirth. As a symbol, the knot is thus charged with significance. In "Complaint," the untying of the knot is followed by a tongue-in-cheek remark about making love that erases one's identity. "I swear, I remember nothing" effectively puts an end to any further questions. See the note (p. 107) on the poem "The Ways of Love."

Here is an anonymous poem, "The Pledge" (p. 8), from *Amaru's One Hundred Poems*, that speaks about separation in love.

He's broken the pledge, banished me
from his heart where I held a special place.
No more in love, he now walks past me
like any other man. The days go by
as I keep thinking of this over and over again.
Dear friend, I don't know why my heart
doesn't break into a hundred pieces.[21]

The woman's lover has not kept faith with her; he has, in fact, abandoned her. When he passes her in the street, he fails to recognize her; she has become a complete stranger. She is heartbroken. He is on her mind night and day, and she does not know what to do. In her loneliness, she confides to her friend and wonders why she is not dead from a broken heart. In fewer than thirty words in the original Sanskrit, the poem tells us all that there is to know about unrequited love. It is a man's world; he does what he pleases. The woman is usually helpless.

Given the nature of Indian patriarchy, it is not unusual for a woman writer to hide her name and gender. Anonymity offered her a refuge from the prying eyes of men. Virginia Woolf (1882–1941) was probably right when she said, "Anon, who wrote so many poems without signing them, was often a woman."[22] It is not improbable that a woman wrote "The Pledge."

The Sanskrit poem begins on an ominous note, *gate premābandhe* (literally, "the bond of love is broken"), that is heartrending. The word *gate* (broken) falls on the ear with the force of a sledgehammer. It is all over between them. There is nothing more to be said. The rest of the poem is just a gloss on this phrase.

There is no such thing as a word-for-word or even a line-by-line translation. By attempting to be faithful to the original, the translation often fails to do justice to the poem. I have tried to make Anon's distinctive voice heard in English by laboring to get the tone right. The result is an equivalent poem in English. The translation conveys, I hope, the woman's helplessness when confronted with the enormity of her lover's betrayal. Of the fifty-six words that make up the English poem, forty-three are monosyllables, suggesting thereby the speaker's bewilderment and inability to fully spell out the magnitude of her loss.

Compare "The Pledge" with Ezra Pound's (1885–1972) "The Jewel Stairs' Grievance" (1915), a translation of a poem by Li Bai (701–762).

> The jewelled steps are already quite white with dew,
> It is so late that the dew soaks my gauze stockings,
> And I let down the crystal curtain
> And watch the moon through the clear autumn.[23]

Pound's comment on the poem is instructive: "Jewel stairs, therefore a palace. Grievance, therefore there is something to complain of. Gauze stockings, therefore a court lady, not a servant who complains. Clear autumn, therefore he has no excuse on account of weather. Also she has come early, for the dew has not merely whitened the stairs, but has soaked her stockings. The poem is especially prized because she utters no direct reproach."[24] The lady is probably one of the imperial concubines in whom the emperor is no longer interested; therefore he doesn't show up. The woman in the Sanskrit poem talks freely and openly about her situation: "He's broken the pledge, banished me/from his heart . . ." The woman in the Chinese poem is, on the other hand, reluctant to speak about her situation. Not one word of reproach escapes her lips. What is unusual about the poem is its admirable restraint. By saying little, it says it all. The images—"jewelled steps," "white with dew," "gauze stockings," "crystal curtain," "clear autumn"—offer the reader, through the power of suggestion, a road map to the situation in the poem: the lady's disappointment in love.

The Sanskrit poets left no aspect of love untouched. There are even a few poems on the unorthodox woman-on-top position (*viparītarata*). Here is an example, "Who Needs the Gods?" (p. 2), from *Amaru's One Hundred Poems*:

With her tangled hair in disarray,
her earrings swinging wildly,
and sweat wiping off the mark on her forehead,
the lovely woman's eyes droop
from the fatigue of riding her lover.
Long may her face protect you.
Brahmā, Viṣṇu, and Śiva—
who needs the gods now?[25]

The *Kāmasūtra* recommends the woman-on-top position when the man is exhausted from lovemaking, when the woman's passion has not subsided, and when a pleasant diversion from the normal position is desired (2.8.1–6). Vātsyāyana explains that with flowers falling from her hair, with laughter interrupted by panting, the woman should pin her lover down and press him with her breasts. In this position, the woman conquers and subdues her man. The poem contrasts sensual pleasures with liberation. While the hermit shuns sensual pleasures for the sake of experiencing divine bliss, the lover shuns divine bliss for the sake of experiencing sensual pleasures. Note the irreverent, almost blasphemous, tone of the speaker. Jayadeva's (12th cent.) *The Love Song of Kṛṣṇa* (*Gītagovinda*) describes Rādhā making love to Kṛṣṇa in this position: "Why do women in love take delight/in the superior position?"[26]

Courtesans in ancient Greece offered this position, known as *kelēs* (the racehorse), only to their wealthy clients. The Greek Anthology furnishes many examples. Here is one, "Doris," by Dioscorides of Alexandria (3rd cent. B.C.E.):

Stretching out the rose-assed Doris on the bed
  I became an immortal in her blooming flowers.
For she, straddling the middle of me with her extraordinary feet
  completed without swerving the marathon of Venus,
looking languidly out of her eyes; but they like leaves in the wind,
  as she rolled around, trembled, crimson,
until the white flow was poured out from both of us
  and Doris was spread loose with limbs relaxed.[27]

See also "She Protests Too Much" (p. 32) and Sonnoka's "Driven by Passion" (p. 87).

Sanskrit poets have long known that the scent of a woman is erotic, as the poem "Who Needs the Gods?" demonstrates. In his *Memoirs*, Giacomo Casanova (1725–1798) makes this observation about erotic scent: "There is something in the air of the bedroom of the woman one loves, something so intimate, so balsamic, such voluptuous emanations, that if a lover had to choose between Heaven and this place of delight, his hesitation would not last for a moment."[28] In both instances, the lovers reject the pleasures of heaven for those of the bedroom.

A woman going out at night to meet her lover (*abhisārikā*) is a popular motif in Sanskrit poetry and drama, as illustrated by the poem "On a Rainy Day" (p. 28), from *A Treasury of Well-Turned Verse*.

Fortunate is the lover who helps his mistress
to change clothes when she comes over on a rainy day.
The kohl around her eyes is washed off by the rain,

and her sheer blue cloth, clinging to her shapely breasts,
reveals the natural beauty of her figure.[29]

The critic Viśvanātha (14th cent.) mentions eight places as being suitable for lovers to meet: a field, a garden, a ruined temple, the house of a female messenger, a grove, an inn, a cremation ground, and the bank of a river.[30] The rainy season (June to September) is especially favored for lovemaking. The classic example of the motif occurs in the fifth act of Śūdraka's play *The Little Clay Cart* (*Mṛcchakaṭika*, 5th cent.), where the heroine, Vasantasenā, sets out at night in the rain to meet her lover, Cārudatta.

Let the clouds burst into rain or thunder
or hurl down lightning bolts from above.
Neither cold nor heat can change the minds
of women setting out to meet their lovers.[31]

The reader witnesses the lover in "On a Rainy Day" undressing his mistress, who is soaked with rain, a prelude to their eventual lovemaking. The pouring rain suggests as much. Nowhere is this motif more persistent than in Bollywood movies where rain-drenched heroines writhe about on the screen, crooning songs. The motif also occurs in Greek poetry—for instance, in "The Unfaithful Wife" by Philodemus of Gadara (ca. 110–30 B.C.E.).

In the middle of the night
I stole from my husband's bed
And came to you, soaked with rain.
And now, are we going to
Sit around, and not get down
To business, and not bill and coo,
And love like lovers ought to love?[32]

Sanskrit poetic convention informs us that if a woman has love on her mind, nothing can stop her. Poem after poem enacts unblushing scenes in which we witness voluptuous women, their hair and clothes in disarray, lying sprawled across beds, exhausted from violent lovemaking.

A genre of Sanskrit poetry is devoted to travelers (*pathikaḥ*) who leave behind wives or lovers as they set out on a journey to seek their fortune. The women do everything in their power to stop them or delay their going away. Often they enlist the services of their girlfriends to persuade their husbands or lovers to change their minds. They are unsuccessful most of the time. In the end, the women reconcile themselves to the situation and fondly look forward to the day when they will be reunited with their loved ones.

The genre first made its appearance in the Prākrit anthology *The Seven Hundred Poems* (*Sattasāī*), compiled by the Sātavāhana king Hāla (1st cent.) of Pratiṣṭhāna (present-day Paithan in Maharashtra). In contrast to Sanskrit, the "well-made" or "refined" language, there were many vernaculars known as Prākrits, the "original" or "natural" languages. One such Prākrit is Pāli, the language of the earliest Buddhist scriptures, the Tipiṭaka (The three baskets, 1st cent. B.C.E.). Let us look at the following poem by Niṣpaṭa (46) from *The Seven Hundred Poems*:

> My heartless lover, I hear,
> is going away tomorrow.
> Grow long, Holy Night, so that
> no tomorrow awaits him.[33]

The young woman prays to the goddess of the night, Rātri, to prevent the day from breaking so that her lover can continue to remain with her instead of going away on a journey. She demands that time itself stop for her. Such extravagant imagery is not unusual in love poems that thrive on hyperbole. Underlying her prayer is the painful reality that time is a reminder of our mortality and that she, like everyone else, is helpless before its omnipotence. She knows all too well that the night will end, and with daybreak her lover will leave home. Her pain, her frustration, and her inability to stop her lover from leaving are concentrated in the word "heartless." In her desperation, she turns to the goddess for help.

There is a flip side to the "traveler" poems. In a few instances, the mistress of the house invites a lonely traveler to spend the night with her when her husband is gone on a journey, as in the following poem by Artha (379), also from *The Seven Hundred Poems*.

With a sneer, the woman had offered
the traveler a straw mat to sleep on;
at dawn she rolls it up, weeping.[34]

The traveler is on his way, having spent the night making love to her. He leaves at dawn, never to return. So the woman weeps. Perhaps they had slept on the same straw mat that she now rolls up. The mat becomes a resonant image that negotiates the transition from "sneer" to "weeping." The traveler's unexpected visit turns the woman's world upside down.

The Sanskrit anthologies continued the tradition initiated by *The Seven Hundred Poems*. Here is an example, "The Traveler" (p. 21), from *The Mark of Love* (*Śṛṅgāratilaka*).

My husband is away on business:
there's been no word from him.
His mother left this morning for her son-in-law's:
her daughter has had a child.
I'm alone and in the full bloom of youth.
How can I meet you tonight?
It is evening. Be on your way, traveler.[35]

A woman invites a traveler to spend the night with her: her husband is "away on business" and her mother-in-law has gone to her son-in-law's. The poem employs a rhetorical figure known as upside-down language—that is, saying one thing and meaning exactly the opposite. By telling the traveler, "Be on your way," she is in fact inviting him into her house. This is one of the few poems in Sanskrit about a wife's infidelity. See also Jaghanacapalā's "Wife" (p. 65) and Vidyā's "The Riverbank" (p. 96). Social conventions prohibit a woman from talking to a stranger. But the speaker in the poem subverts those conventions by indirectly asking the traveler to spend the night with her. Other "traveler" poems in this selection are "An Invitation" (p. 20), Keśaṭa's "The Camel" (p. 70), Morikā's "Don't Go" (p. 78), and Rudraṭa's "What the Young Wife Said to the Traveler" (p. 83).

The parallels between the Prākrit and Sanskrit "traveler" poems, "With a sneer, the woman had offered" and "My husband is away on business," are obvious. The former dispenses with innuendo and double entendre, while the latter revels in them. Shorn of embellishments, the Prākrit poem is more natural in its tone and achieves its effects through ordinary, everyday images, such as a straw mat. The Sanskrit poem is, on the other hand, dramatic; it enacts a little scene and uses all the resources of the language to achieve its effects.

"Traveler" poems are mirror images of poems featuring the *abhisārikā*. In the latter poems, it is the woman, with love on her mind, who sets out under cover of darkness to meet her lover and spend the night with him. In the former, it is the traveler who is invited by the woman into her house to spend the night with her. Both liaisons are illicit and socially disapproved. It is therefore not surprising to find poets writing about illicit love in a society where a woman's chastity is closely guarded, both before and after marriage. Ancient Indian women, like women elsewhere, wanted ownership of their bodies, which patriarchy did everything in its power to deny. Nowhere is the battle of the sexes more valiantly fought than in these little-known stanza poems, some of which have miraculously survived into our own time.

The infidelity of the man often causes separation between the lovers. The woman's pride is hurt and she feels offended. The motif of the offended woman (*māninī*) is a favorite of the poets. There is a dramatic tension to the poems where this motif occurs, as in the poem "She Doesn't Let Go of Her Pride" (p. 33). The separation is not indefinite; the lovers eventually reunite.

She turns aside his eyes,
riveted on her breasts,
by embracing him.
She puts rouge on her lips,

seeing his lips burn for hers.
She stops his hand on her crotch
by closing her thighs tight.
Tactfully, she neither rejects
her husband's love
nor lets go of her pride.[36]

The woman is unable to tell her husband to his face that she is outraged by his infidelity when he returns home after visiting a courtesan. In her helplessness, she tries to punish him by rejecting any intimacy. That is as far as she will go. She simply does not have the power to walk out on her husband when he cheats on her. The motif is a staple of devotional (*bhakti*) poetry, as in the following lines from a Bengali devotional poem, "The Marks of Fingernails Are on Your Breast," by Govindadāsa (16th cent.), where Rādhā cries her heart out at Kṛṣṇa's infidelities:

The marks of fingernails are on your breast
and my heart burns.
Kohl of someone's eyes upon your lips
darkens my face.
I am awake all night.[37]

See also "A Woman Wronged" (p. 16), Mahodadhi's "Stop Being Willful" (p. 77), and Śrīharṣa's "The Smart Girl" (p. 88).

And here is a poem that illustrates both aspects of love, "Then and Now" (p. 86), by Śīlābhaṭṭārikā, a woman poet probably from southern India. The honorific suffix *bhaṭṭārikā* (noble, venerable) points to her distinguished status.

My husband is the same man who stole my virginity.
These are the same moonlit nights;
the same breeze floats down from the Vindhya mountains,
thick with the scent of flowering jasmine.
I too am the same woman. Yet I long with all my heart
for the thicket of reeds by the river
that once knew our wild joyous lovemaking.[38]

This is a justly famous poem; it strikes a personal note, something that one does not often come across in Sanskrit poetry. Hindu scriptures encourage sex as one of the four legitimate aims of life for the householder. In the Hindu view, woman has a far greater erotic disposition than man, and her delight in the sexual act is far greater. A text puts it well: "Want of sexual enjoyment is decay and old age for women."[39] The speaker, who is a woman, contrasts the two stages of her relationship with her man: one, when they were young unmarried lovers, and the other, when they are a middle-aged couple. She recalls with genuine regret their "wild joyous lovemaking" on moonlit nights by the riverside among the "thicket of reeds" with not a care in the world, away from the prying eyes of her family and neighbors. Now marriage, with all the responsibilities it entails, has put out the fires of love.

She reflects on her illicit premarital love, finding it to be far richer and more satisfying than marital love. Coming from a woman poet, this is an extraordinary statement. Implicit in the poem is the recognition that like everything else in the world, love, too, is subject to change—a fact that we find hard to accept. We expect permanence in love. The oneness that she had experienced at first as a lover is not there anymore. Now married, she looks back at that period in their lives and is unhappy. Perhaps her husband is no longer in love with her.

The elements—"moonlit nights" and "breeze"—have not changed, and neither has she. She is still the "same woman," and yet one thing has changed—their love. Not only has time weakened the bonds of love, it has also exposed the fragility of their relationship. It is this knowledge that makes her unhappy. It is impossible to reproduce in English the music of the original Sanskrit. It is a cri de coeur that we are all too familiar with in English poetry and rarely meet with in Sanskrit poetry, which by tradition is impersonal. "Then and Now" has much in common with such poems as the anonymous sixteenth-century English lyric "Western Wind":

> Westron wynde when wyll thow blow
> The smalle rayne downe can rayne—
> Cryst, yf my love wer in my armys
> And I in my bed agayne![40]

In Sanskrit erotic poetry, it is the male voice that we invariably hear. But Śīlābhaṭṭārikā speaks in a recognizable woman's voice that affects us deeply. She speaks not only for herself but also for all women. That is the poem's enduring appeal.

ASCETICISM

Renouncing the world to devote oneself to one's liberation is, like sensual pleasures, one of the four legitimate aims of life. The renouncer leaves his family behind and lives the life of a wandering hermit.

More than any other poet in our selection, Bhartṛhari (ca. 400 C.E.), in his *Three Hundred Poems* (*Śatakatrayādi-subhāṣitasaṃgrah*), famously wrestled with the situation of the hermit. He is keenly aware that all things pass, that nothing, especially sensual pleasures, is permanent. Even as he enjoys the moment, he seems to regret it. It is this awareness that makes his verse so poignant. Though he knows that sensual pleasures are fleeting, he abandons himself to them while they last. Sensual pleasures are, for Bhartṛhari, embodied in women; he speaks again and again of the pleasures that a woman's body offers. But women in his poems are inert objects, images that he fondly gazes on. Though his eyes see the "skull beneath the skin," he is unable to withdraw his gaze. This conflict is at the heart of Bhartṛhari's poetry, as in the poem "Wise Men" (p. 43):

> In this shallow fickle world,
> wise men choose two courses:
> for a time they keep the company of minds
> steeped in the ocean of wisdom.
> They spend the rest with nubile young women
> whose full hips and breasts
> glow with the pleasure of hiding
> men's impatient hands
> in the depths of their thighs.[41]

The poem overwhelms us by its assault on the senses; it presents images of women's breasts, hips, and thighs, all waiting to be aroused by "men's impatient hands." The foreplay suggests the possibility of eventual consummation, which is not explicitly spelled out. Bhartṛhari leaves it to the reader's imagination to complete the scene. Every brushstroke of this erotic scene is dictated by tradition. Yet Bhartṛhari goes beyond tradition by speaking of sensual pleasures in the same breath as the pursuit of self-knowledge that would ultimately lead to liberation. He does not privilege one over the other. He presents us with the reality of man's predicament. Given the options, few men would care to "keep the company of minds/ steeped in the ocean of wisdom" when the alternative is so much more attractive. Philosophical poet that he is, he sees the value of sensual pleasures and of its polar opposite, liberation. This opposition is built into the Hindu tradition itself that Bhartṛhari's poetry interrogates. The situation makes for tension that is reflected in the uneasy tone. It is tone that accounts for the force of the poem.

Like Bhartṛhari, Asclepiades, too, mourns the impermanence of sensual pleasures. The speaker in the poem "To His Mistress" urges his companion to give herself up to him since there are "no lovers . . . in the underworld."

> You deny me: and to what end?
> There are no lovers, dear, in the underworld,
> No love but here: only the living know
> The sweetness of Aphrodite—
>   but below,
> But in Acheron, careful virgin, dust and ashes
> Will be our only lying down together.[42]

But Bhartṛhari takes the epigram one step further by using the occasion for philosophic reflection. He is enough of a pragmatist who accepts the human need for sensual pleasures but is aware that he needs to move beyond them. He does not of course see sensual pleasures as an obstacle to liberation; he goes against tradition in this respect. Considering the times he lived in, his thinking is revolutionary. He is unrivaled by any other Sanskrit lyric poet with the exception of Kālidāsa. See also Bhartṛhari's "Hips" (p. 46). His is a unique voice in Sanskrit poetry.

A characteristic that Bhartṛhari's poems share with those of Asclepiades is that both poets cast their poems as epigrams. The poems are short, concrete, and often ironic. The highly inflected nature of Sanskrit and Greek makes possible an unusual conciseness of expression. The poems of Bhartṛhari and Asclepiades are classic examples of the genre.

Sanskrit poets had an endless fascination with woman's body, which they invariably described through a series of conventional images. Bhartṛhari ridicules such poets in his poem "Adoration of Woman" (p. 49) for following tradition blindly and for not being innovative enough in their use of imagery:

Those lumps of flesh, her breasts,
are compared to golden bowls.
That storehouse of phlegm, her face,
is compared to the moon.
Damp with urine, her thigh
is said to surpass the elephant's trunk.
Look how poets embellish her vile body.[43]

Even Kālidāsa was not above using stock images. Bhartṛhari raises an important critical issue here: the Sanskrit poet's utter subservience to tradition even at the expense of his own creativity. Often, one poem is no different from another. Bhartṛhari is a fine example of a poet who does not fall into this category. His poetry constantly surprises us with its wit and inventiveness, much as John Donne's (1572–1631) poetry does, as in these lines from "Elegy 19: To His Mistress Going to Bed" (1669):

Full nakedness! All joys are due to thee,
As souls unbodied, bodies unclothed must be
To taste whole joys . . .
                                        Cast all, yea, this white linen hence,
Here is no penance, much less innocence.[44]

Donne, too, like Bhartṛhari, was troubled by the need for sensual pleasures and wished to move beyond them. His poetry suggests as much.

Long before Bhartṛhari, poets had wrestled with this conflict. Here is an example, "Song of a Former Prostitute," by Vimalā, from the Pāli *Songs of the Elder Nuns* (*Therīgāthā*, 6th–3rd cent. B.C.E.).

Young and overbearing—
drunk with fame, with beauty,
with my figure, its flawless appearance—
I held other women in contempt.

Heavily made-up, I leaned
against the brothel door
and flashed my wares. Like a hunter,
I laid my snares to surprise fools.

I even taught them a trick or two
as I slipped my clothes off
and bared my secret places.
O how I despised them!

Today, head shaved, wrapped
in a single robe, an almswoman,
I move about or sit at the foot
of a tree, empty of all thoughts.

All ties to heaven and earth
I have cut loose forever.
Uprooting every obsession,
I have put out the fires.[45]

The Pāli Buddhist poets replaced the profane language of the Sanskrit poets with a sacred one. They abandoned the love poetry of the Sanskrit poets and replaced it with a poetry that speaks of liberation from the cycle of birth, death, and rebirth, the perfect bliss that was sought by every Buddhist monk and nun. This is entirely in keeping with the teachings of the Buddha, which consider sexual desire an obstacle to enlightenment.

Nowhere is this idea more forcefully stated than in the *Aṅguttara Nikāya* (Gradual sayings, 1.1): "Monks, I know of no other form that so captivates the mind of a man than the form of a woman. I know of no other voice, no other scent, no other taste, no other touch that so captivates the mind of a man as the voice, the scent, the taste, the touch of a woman."[46] While Bhartṛhari accepts sensual pleasures, impermanent as they are, Vimalā rejects them as an obstacle to enlightenment. Her response is entirely in keeping with tradition.

It is said that Sanskrit poetry is impersonal—that is, the poet has taken himself out of the situation in the poem and speaks to us not directly but through a persona. Specifics are omitted; so are the names of individuals. With the erasure of all particulars, the situation is represented as the distillation of a universal human experience that evokes a single mood such as the erotic or the heroic. The poem itself follows the established conventions of poetics, though occasionally it breaks out of them to explore new possibilities. Bhartṛhari stands at the crossroads of tradition and innovation. Herein lies his enduring appeal and the reason why he is able to speak to us.

NATURE

Let us look at the following lines from "I Built My Hut," a poem by Tao Qian (ca. 365–427), also known as Tao Yuanming:

> I pluck chrysanthemums under the eastern hedge,
> Then gaze long at the distant summer hills.
> The mountain air is fresh at the dusk of day:
> The flying birds two by two return.
> In these things there lies a deep meaning;
> Yet when we would express it, words suddenly fail us.[47]

The poet is alone, contemplating a natural scene from his home overlooking Mount Lu in Jiangxi province in southeastern China. There is a hint of intimacy between him and the scene that holds a meaning for him that cannot be put into words. The Daoist classic *Daodejing* (The Way and its power, 4th–3rd cent. B.C.E.), says as much: "One who knows does not speak; one who speaks does not know."[48] We notice in Tao's poem the absence of pathetic fallacy—that is, endowing nature with human qualities, which informs much of English Romantic poetry.

Unlike Chinese poetry, where images of the natural world often appear, Sanskrit poetry contains few references to nature. The Sanskrit poets were usually patronized by kings and lived in cities such as Ujjayinī (Ujjain in Madhya Pradesh) and Kānyakubja (Kannauj in Uttar Pradesh). Country scenes were not to their taste, and therefore they figured infrequently in their poetry. There are, however, some exceptions, notably Yogeśvara (ca. 800–900) and Abhinanda (ca. 850–900), who were both from Bengal. Here is a poem, "When the Rains Come" (p. 100), by the former.

> The river overflowing its banks fills my heart with delight:
> on top of a canebrake, a snake is asleep;
> a moorhen calls out; geese clamor;
> herds of deer gather in knots;
> the thick grass is weighed down by streams of ants;
> and the jungle fowl is drunk with joy.[49]

Yogeśvara has a gift for describing country scenes realistically—that is, describing "things as they are." The poet's observant eye scans the countryside and fondly records every detail of the scene that comes to life with the monsoon. Like the "jungle fowl," the speaker, too, is overjoyed. But the poem stops there. It makes no attempt to evaluate the experience of "delight" that the speaker feels. Man and nature are not one, as in the Chinese poem, as a result of their encounter. Nor do we come across here anything like the impassioned personal utterance of a Wordsworth (1770–1850), as in the following passage from "Lines Composed a Few Miles Above Tintern Abbey" (1798):

> . . . And I have felt
> A presence that disturbs me with the joy
> Of elevated thoughts; a sense sublime

Of something far more deeply interfused,
Whose dwelling is the light of setting suns,
And the round ocean and the living air,
And the blue sky, and in the mind of man . . .[50]

As a poet writing within a tradition that demanded formal perfection, Yogeśvara did not succumb entirely to the tyranny of form. His few poems on country scenes are a breath of fresh air.[51] Abhinanda praises his realism:

Words blossomed when Yogeśvara spoke
of the Revā and the Vindhya,
of Pulīndra and Pāmara women,
and of a message drifting through a storm.[52]

ANONYMITY

In "Status of Indian Women," the influential art historian Ananda K. Coomaraswamy (1877–1947) observed, "[Anonymity] is one of the proudest distinctions of the Hindu culture. The names of the 'authors' of the epics are but shadows, and in later ages it was a constant practice of writers to suppress their own names and ascribe their work to a mythical or famous poet, thereby to gain a better attention for the truth that they would rather claim to have 'heard' than to have 'made.'"[53] Much of Sanskrit poetry that has survived is anonymous. We know it only from medieval anthologies that began to appear in print in the nineteenth century (see "Notes," pp. 123–125). We know now that "Kālidāsa" and "Bhavabhūti" are not the real names of these poets; they are pseudonyms.

The practice of naming a poet by an epithet from his or her poem was fairly common. Take the name Karṇotpala, for instance. The epithet occurs in the poem "The Lamp" (p. 69): "She then hurled at the lamp the lotus from her ear/and put out the quivering flame." The poet is known only by his epithet: "[The Poet of] the Lotus from the Ear." We do not know his real name. This is his only poem that has survived. Likewise, Bhavabhūti is so named because it is believed that the god Śiva (Bhava) offered him "holy ashes," or "luck" (*bhūti*). His name would therefore mean "[The Poet Who Was] Blessed by Śiva." His real name was, however, Śrīkaṇṭha Nīlakaṇṭha Udumbara, where Śrīkaṇṭha means "one in whose throat dwells the goddess of eloquence." Siegfried Lienhard has an interesting take on the Sanskrit poets' use of pseudonyms: "Whereas pseudonyms in Western literature are designed to give anonymity, the names chosen by Indian *kavis* [poets] are taken not to hide their identity but to refer to the glory, rank, or some particular gift possessed by the poet."[54]

Two women poets are known by somewhat unusual epithets: Jaghanacapalā (A Woman Who Wiggles Her Bottom) and Vikaṭanitambā (A Woman with a Fat Rump). Both names appear to be fictitious, since no women, except prostitutes, would have such names.

POETS AND THEIR PATRONS

Long before Bhartṛhari, Sanskrit had ceased to be a spoken language and had become primarily a literary language that flourished in the courts under the patronage of kings. Poets traveled far and wide in search of patrons. They regarded themselves as the sole custodians of the word and seldom deferred to the authority of kings. Often they fell out with their patrons, as the following poem, "The Poet Speaks to the King" (p. 50) by Bhartṛhari, indicates.

> You are a lord of riches; words obey my call.
> You are a man of arms;
> my undying eloquence vanquishes pride.
> Those blinded by wealth slave for you,
> but they are eager to hear me
> to rid their minds of evil.
> Since you have no respect for me, king,
> I respect you even less. I shall leave.[55]

A few poets have been at odds with the state. The classic example is the Russian Jewish poet Osip Mandelstam (1891–1938), whose poem "The Stalin Epigram" (composed November 1933), in which he made fun of the Soviet dictator, led to his arrest the following year and to eventual deportation to Kolyma in Siberia for "counterrevolutionary activities." Mandelstam's contempt for Stalin is evident in these lines:

> But whenever there's a snatch of talk
> it turns to the Kremlin mountaineer,
>
> the ten thick worms his fingers,
> his words like measures of weight,
>
> the huge laughing cockroaches on his top lip,
> the glitter of his boot-rims.[56]

Bhartṛhari is not as brutal as Mandelstam in his denunciation of the king. Empowered with "undying eloquence," he shows the king his place. Respecting the king "even less," he leaves. He is not one to trade his self-respect for patronage, even if the patron is a "lord of riches."

Not all poets had such confrontational relationships with their patrons. The Tamil poet Auvaiyār (2nd–3rd cent.) mourns the death of her patron Atiyamāṉ Neṭumāṉ Añci in battle in some of the most memorable poems in the language, as in these lines from the poem "But That Time Has Passed Now":

> The spear, that pierced his chest and dropped,
> also pierced the hands of the many who came to him seeking
>   alms;
> it pierced the wide bowls of great, incomparable bards;
> it pierced the tongues of poets, skilled in putting words
>   together,
> and blurred the pupils in the sorrowful eyes of those who
>   depended on him.
> Where is he now, our lord and main support?[57]

Poets depended on kings for their livelihood; kings depended on poets to spread their fame and glory in undying song.

The following anecdote, from a biography of the medieval poet Harihara (13th cent.), tells us how frustrating the relationship between the poet and his patron can sometimes be:

> Lord! Where does a man go? Where does he lie down?
> Whom does he speak to? And to whom recite his poems?
> Where does he pursue undisturbed the art of poetry?
> At whose court does he solicit?
> Wicked fools have taken over the world, and there is nothing
> the wise Harihara, who knows the truth, can do about it.[58]

Disenchanted with life, Harihara renounces the world and becomes a monk. Bhartṛhari, as we have seen, exemplifies this tendency more than any other poet.

"Without scholarship, no classical text could survive and be read," observed the classicist D. S. Carne-Ross, "but scholarship alone cannot preserve a poet as a vital presence. That is the task of poets and good readers of poetry from generation to generation."[59] I hope that "poets and good readers of poetry" will ensure the survival of these breathtaking poems from the Sanskrit, albeit in translation, which has offered them an afterlife in another language. Sanskrit poetry, like Greek and Latin poetry, is our common inheritance.

NOTES

1. Daniel H. H. Ingalls, trans., *An Anthology of Sanskrit Court Poetry: Vidyākara's "Subhāṣitaratnakoṣa,"* Harvard Oriental Series 44 (Cambridge, Mass.: Harvard University Press, 1965).
2. John Brough, trans., *Poems from the Sanskrit* (Harmondsworth, U.K.: Penguin, 1968).
3. W. S. Merwin and J. Moussaieff Masson, trans., *Sanskrit Love Poetry* (New York: Columbia University Press, 1977).

4. Barbara Stoler Miller, trans., *The Hermit and the Love-Thief: Sanskrit Poems of Bhartrihari and Bilhaṇa* (New York: Columbia University Press, 1978).
5. Martha Ann Selby, trans. and ed., *Grow Long, Blessed Night: Love Poems from Classical India* (New York: Oxford University Press, 2000).
6. *Love Lyrics by Amaru, Bhartṛhari, and Bilhaṇa*, trans. Greg Bailey and Richard Gombrich, Clay Sanskrit Library (New York: New York University Press; John and Jennifer Clay Foundation, 2005).
7. Kumārajīva, quoted in Martha P. Y. Cheung, ed., *An Anthology of Chinese Discourse on Translation, Volume 1: From Earliest Times to the Buddhist Project* (Manchester, U.K.: St Jerome, 2006), 1:94.
8. RV 7.87.4, in *Der Rig-Veda: Aus dem Sanskrit ins Deutsche übersetzt und mit einem laufenden Kommentar versehen von Karl Friedrich Geldner*, ed. and trans. Karl Friedrich Geldner, 4 vols., Harvard Oriental Series 33–36 (Cambridge, Mass.: Harvard University Press, 1951–1957). See pages 127–128 in the present volume for a list of abbreviations.
9. *Kavikaṇṭhābharaṇa* of Kṣemendra, ed. Pandit Dhundhiraja Sastri (Banaras: Chaukhamba Sanskrit Series Office, 1933), vols. 10, 11. Quoted in Merwin and Masson, *Sanskrit Love Poetry*, 5–6. The translation is by Merwin.
10. *Kāvyamīmāṃsa* of Rājaśekhara, rev. K. S. Ramaswami Sastri Siromani, Gaekwad's Oriental Series, no. 1, 3rd ed. (1916; repr., Baroda: Oriental Institute, Maharaja Sayajirao University of Baroda, 1934).
11. A. Berriedale Keith, preface to *A History of Sanskrit Literature* (London: Oxford University Press, 1920), vii. Quoted in Brough, *Poems from the Sanskrit*, 20.
12. Sheldon Pollock, "Sanskrit Literary Culture from the Inside Out," in *Literary Cultures in History: Reconstructions from South Asia*, ed. Sheldon Pollock, 39–130 (Berkeley: University of California Press, 2003), and Sheldon Pollock, *The Language of the Gods in the World of Men: Sanskrit, Culture, and Power in Premodern India* (Berkeley: University of California Press, 2006).
13. AS 107, in *Amaruśataka*, with the Sanskrit commentary the *Rasikasañjīvinī* of Arjunavarmadeva, ed. Pandit Durgaprasad and Kasinath Pandurang Parab (Bombay: Nirnaya Sagara Press, 1889), 71.

14. *Amaruśataka*, with the Sanskrit commentary the *Śṛṅgāradīpikā* of Vemabhūpāla, ed. and trans. Chintaman Ramchandra Devadhar (1959; repr., New Delhi: Motilal Banarsidass, 1984), 80.
15. Alain Daniélou, trans., *The Complete Kāma Sūtra: The First Unabridged Modern Translation of the Classic Indian Text* (Rochester, Vt.: Park Street Press, 1994).
16. G. B. Mohan Thampi, "Rasa as Aesthetic Experience," *Journal of Aesthetics and Art Criticism* 24, no. 1 (1965): 78.
17. *The Bible: Authorized King James Version*, introduction and notes by Robert Carroll and Stephen Prickett, Oxford World's Classics (Oxford: Oxford University Press, 1997), 728.
18. *Anaṅgaraṅga* of Kalyāṇamalla, ed., with a Hindi translation and commentary, by Ram Sagar Tripathi (Delhi: Chaukhamba Sanskrit Pratishthan, 1988), 224.
19. VSR 574, in *Subhāṣitaratnakoṣa*, comp. Vidyākara, ed. D. D. Kosambi and V. V. Gokhale, Harvard Oriental Series 42 (Cambridge, Mass.: Harvard University Press, 1957), 105.
20. Sherod Santos, trans., *Greek Lyric Poetry: A New Translation* (New York: Norton, 2005), 94.
21. AS 43, in Durgaprasad and Parab, *Amaruśataka*, 38.
22. Virginia Woolf, *A Room of One's Own* (San Diego: Harcourt, Brace, Jovanovich, 1957), 51.
23. Ezra Pound, "The Jewel Stairs' Grievance," in *Translations* (New York: New Directions, 1963), 194.
24. "Note," ibid.
25. AS 3, in Durgaprasad and Parab, *Amaruśataka*, 6.
26. *Love Song of the Dark Lord: Jayadeva's "Gītagovinda,"* ed. and trans. Barbara Stoler Miller (New York: Columbia University Press, 1977), 166.
27. Amy Richlin, *The Garden of Priapus: Sexuality and Aggression in Roman Humor* (New Haven, Conn.: Yale University Press, 1983), 50.
28. Giacomo Casanova, quoted in Havelock Ellis, *Studies in the Psychology of Sex, Volume 4: Sexual Selection in Man* (Philadelphia: Davis, 1914), 78.
29. VSR 261, in Kosambi and Gokhale, *Subhāṣitaratnakoṣa*, 48.

30. *Sāhityadarpaṇa* of Śrī Viśvanātha Kavirāja, ed., with a commentary, by Pandit Sri Krishna Mohan Thakur, Kashi Sanskrit Series 145, 3rd ed. (Varanasi: Chaukhamba Sanskrit Series Office, 1967), 3:80.
31. *Mṛcchakaṭika* of Śūdraka, ed., with the commentary of Pṛthvīdhara, by Kasinath Pandurang Parab, rev. Vasudev Laksman Sastri Pansikar, 6th ed. (Bombay: Nirnaya Sagara Press, 1926), 124.
32. Kenneth Rexroth, trans., *Poems from the Greek Anthology* (Ann Arbor: University of Michigan Press, 1962), 93.
33. *Das Saptaçatakam des Hâla*, ed. Albrecht Weber, Abhandlungen für die Kunde des Morgenlandes, Band 7, No. 4 (Leipzig: Brockhaus, 1881), 17.
34. Ibid., 145.
35. *Ṛtusaṃhāra*, including the commentary of Maṇirāma, and *Śṛṅgāratilaka*, ed. Vasudev Laksman Sastri Pansikar, 4th ed. (Bombay: Nirnaya Sagara Press, 1913), 3.
36. VSR 690, in Kosambi and Gokhale, *Subhāṣitaratnakoṣa*, 126.
37. Edward C. Dimock Jr. and Denise Levertov, trans., *In Praise of Krishna: Songs from the Bengali* (Garden City, N.Y.: Doubleday, 1967), 45.
38. VSR 815, in Kosambi and Gokhale, *Subhāṣitaratnakoṣa*, 150.
39. Quoted in Johann Jakob Meyer, *Sexual Life in Ancient India: A Study in the Comparative History of Indian Culture*, 2 vols. (London: Routledge and Kegan Paul, 1930), 1:229.
40. Paul Keegan, ed., *The New Penguin Book of English Verse* (London: Penguin, 2001), 74.
41. BS 88, in *Śatakatrayādi-subhāṣitasaṃgraḥ* of Bhartṛhari, ed. D. D. Kosambi, Singhi Jain Series, no. 23 (Bombay: Bharatiya Vidya Bhavan, 1948), 35.
42. Dudley Fitts, trans., *Poems from the Greek Anthology* (New York: New Directions, 1938), 35.
43. BS 159, in Kosambi, *Śatakatrayādi-subhāṣitasaṃgraḥ* of Bhartṛhari, 62.
44. John Donne, "Elegy 19: To His Mistress Going to Bed," in *John Donne's Poetry*, ed. Arthur L. Clements, 2nd ed. (New York: Norton, 1992), 62.
45. *Thera- and Therī-Gāthā: Stanzas Ascribed to Elders of the Buddhist Order of Recluses*, ed. Hermann Oldenburg and Richard Pischel, Pāli Text Society, 2nd ed. (London: Luzac, 1966), 131.

46. Quoted in H. W. Schumann, *The Historical Buddha*, trans. M. O'C. Walshe (London: Arkana, 1989), 208.
47. Arthur Waley, trans., *Translations from the Chinese* (New York: Knopf, 1941), 83.
48. *Lao Tzu: Tao Te Ching*, trans. D. C. Lau (Harmondsworth, U.K.: Penguin, 1963), 117.
49. VSR 221, in Kosambi and Gokhale, *Subhāṣitaratnakoṣa*, 42.
50. William Wordsworth, "Lines Composed a Few Miles Above Tintern Abbey," in *Selected Poems*, ed. John O. Hayden (London: Penguin, 1994), 68.
51. See Daniel H. H. Ingalls, "A Sanskrit Poetry of Village and Field: Yogeśvara and His Fellow Poets," *Journal of the American Oriental Society* 74, no. 3 (July–September 1954): 119–31.
52. VSR 1699, in Kosambi and Gokhale, *Subhāṣitaratnakoṣa*, 293.
53. Ananda K. Coomaraswamy, "Status of Indian Women," in *The Dance of Shiva: Fourteen Indian Essays*, rev. ed. (New York: Noonday Press, 1956), 102.
54. Siegfried Lienhard, *A History of Classical Poetry: Sanskrit, Pāli, Prākrit*, A History of Indian Literature, vol. 3, fasc. 1, ed. Jan Gonda (Wiesbaden: Harrassowitz, 1984), 189, n. 106.
55. BS 166, in Kosambi, *Śatakatrayādi-subhāṣitasaṃgrah* of Bhartṛhari, 65.
56. Clarence Brown and W. S. Merwin, trans., *The Selected Poems of Osip Mandelstam* (New York: New York Review Books, 2004), 69–70.
57. PN 235, in *Puṟanāṉūṟu*, comp. Peruntēvaṉār, ed. Auvai Cu. Turaicamippillai, 2 vols. (Tirunelveli: South India Saivasiddhanta Publishing Works Society, 1967–1972), 2:76.
58. RP 12.11, in *Prabandhakoṣa* of Rājaśekhara Sūri, ed., with a Hindi translation, by Jina Vijaya, Singhi Jain Series, no. 6 (Santiniketan, West Bengal: Adhisthata-Singhi Jaina Jnanapitha, 1935), 61.
59. D. S. Carne-Ross, *Pindar* (New Haven, Conn.: Yale University Press, 1985), 5–6.

EROTIC POEMS FROM THE SANSKRIT

ABHINANDA

THAT'S HOW I SAW HER

Hurriedly, she threw my silk cloth over her loins
and knotted her hair that had come loose
in the vigorous love play; her heavy breathing
showed my fingernail marks on her breasts.
That's how I saw her, head lowered,
recalling her boldness, after we had made love.

AMARU

WHO NEEDS THE GODS?

With her tangled hair in disarray,
her earrings swinging wildly,
and sweat wiping off the mark on her forehead,
the lovely woman's eyes droop
from the fatigue of riding her lover.
Long may her face protect you.
Brahmā, Viṣṇu, and Śiva—
who needs the gods now?

IN A HUNDRED PLACES

When my face turned to meet his,
I lowered my eyes and stared at my feet.
When my ears longed to hear him talk,
I kept them shut tight.
When my cheeks, damp with sweat, flushed red,
I covered them with my hands.
But what could I do, friends,
when the seams of my bodice
tore in a hundred places?

A TASTE OF AMBROSIA

She was startled when he bit her lower lip.
Shaking her finger at him, she yelled,
"Stop it! Let go of me, you rogue!"
Her anger rose to fever pitch:
her slender eyebrows danced
and her eyes rolled, as she drew her breath.
Whoever has kissed such a high-toned woman
has tasted ambrosia, for which
the foolish gods churned the ocean.

PINCERS

“The bed is rough and itchy, my love,
from the sandalwood powder
scattered by our tight embrace.”
He said this and made me sit on his chest,
and bit my lips hard in excitement.
The rogue even pulled my clothes off
with his toes, working them like pincers.
Later, he did just as he pleased with me.

THE BRIDE

With a trembling hand, she reaches for her clothes,
tosses the remains of her garland at the burning lamp;
coyly she smiles and covers her husband's eyes
with her hands. Such is the ravishing sight
he comes upon every time they've made love.

ANON

LOVERS' QUARREL

Miserable and unwilling to talk,
they lay on the bed, faces turned away;
though in their hearts they wished
to make it up, pride stood in the way.
Then, slowly, out of the corner of their eyes,
each caught a glimpse of the other.
The quarrel ended in a burst of laughter
as they turned around and hugged each other.

THE PLEDGE

He's broken the pledge, banished me
from his heart where I held a special place.
No more in love, he now walks past me
like any other man. The days go by
as I keep thinking of this over and over again.
Dear friend, I don't know why my heart
doesn't break into a hundred pieces.

A LOVER'S WELCOME

She hung a broad festoon above the door—
with only her eyes, not with blue lotuses.
She gave away a bunch of flowers—
with only her smiles, not with jasmine and such.
She made a ritual offering—
with only the sweat trickling down her breasts,
not with water splashed from a jar.
And with only her body,
the lovely woman welcomed her lover into the house.

REGRET

"Fool! Why didn't I caress my lord's neck?
Why did I lower my face when he kissed me?
Why didn't I look at him? Speak to him?"
The young wife, now seasoned in love's delights,
regrets her naive ways as a new bride.

STONEHEARTED

On merely hearing his name,
a shiver runs through my body.
At the very sight of his face,
I break out in a sweat like a moonstone.

When my lover, who is dearer to me
than life itself, comes near and caresses
my neck, I stop sulking, though at times
I am as stonehearted as ever.

FEIGNING SLEEP

Seeing that she was unattended in the bedroom,
the young wife rose slowly from the bed
and looked long at her husband's face
as he feigned sleep. Boldly she kissed him
but noticing his flushed cheeks,
lowered her head in shame.
Her loved one then burst out laughing
and for long covered her face with kisses.

REMORSE

My face is etched in sorrow;
my heart's uprooted; I am sleepless
and worn out weeping day and night
from not seeing my lover's face;
my body's wasted away.
Contrite, he had groveled at my feet,
yet I had spurned him.
Friends, were you looking out for me
when I exploded at him in anger?

WALKING THE STREET BY HER HOUSE

Just a glimpse of her blows his mind away
and he thinks of a ruse to make her acquaintance.
When passion reaches fever pitch,
he will have to approach a friend to help out.
Short of the pleasure of embracing his love,
even walking the street by her house
makes him delirious with joy.

THE SHEETS

Smudged here with betel juice, burnished there
with aloe paste, a splash of powder in one corner,
and lac from footprints painted in another,
with flowers from her hair strewn all over
its winding crumpled folds, the sheets celebrate
the woman's pleasure of making love in every position.

A WOMAN WRONGED

No, she didn't slam the door in his face
nor turn away from him.
Not a harsh word crossed her lips.
Her gaze unwavering, eyelashes still,
she looked at her husband
as though he were an ordinary man.

AUBADE

The fever of passion spent but nipples still erect
from her husband's tight embrace,
the young woman at daybreak views her body
that had given him such pleasure,
and smiling to herself leaves the bedroom.

LIKE THE WHEELS OF A CHARIOT

I, Yamī, am overcome by love for Yama.
I long to sleep with him in the same bed,
to open my body as a wife would to her husband.
Like the wheels of a chariot, may we move as one.

THE WORD

One who looks does not see the word;
one who listens does not hear it.
As a wife in beautiful clothes
reveals her body to her husband,
so does the word reveal itself to you.

AN INVITATION

"Won't you lie down for a while
in this thicket of reeds and bamboo trees
and look at this field here?"
Even as the girl herding cows
said this to the young traveler,
casually sitting by the roadside,
a shiver ran through her body.

THE TRAVELER

My husband's away on business:
there's been no word from him.
His mother left this morning for her son-in-law's:
her daughter has had a child.
I'm alone and in the full bloom of youth.
How can I meet you tonight?
It is evening. Be on your way, traveler.

THE DEVOTED WIFE

It would be unlucky if I say, "Don't go."
"By all means go," would be heartless.
"Stay beside me," overbearing.
"Do as you please," the height of indifference.
You may or may not believe me if I say,
"I won't live without you."
Teach me the right thing to say, my lord,
when you leave this world.

THE KINGDOM'S HAPPINESS

Though I conquer the whole world,
in truth, there is only one city;
in that city, only one house;
in that house, only one room;
in that room, only one bed;
in that bed, glowing like a jewel,
only one woman—
the source of the kingdom's happiness.

HAIR

Once untied my woman's hair tumbles down,
damp, filling the air with perfume,
only to be tied again before it clings to her loins,
burnt by the white flow of passion.

WILD NIGHTS

This much I know: I trembled like a vine
when he took me in his arms,
when he fondled my breasts and wouldn't let go,
when he tossed aside the garland.
That's all I remember, friend.
Of what happened next—the body going limp,
breath fluttering—I recall nothing.

THANK OFFERING

We leave our youth behind with each passing day:
fuck me always so long as you have the strength.
For once you're dead, my love, who will offer you,
as you lie on a bed of kusa grass,
with sesame and water, a smooth shaven cunt?

AT THE CREMATION GROUND

A poor man hurries to the cremation ground
and pleads with a corpse: "Rise and carry
for just a moment, friend, this heavy burden of poverty
that I may enjoy forever your death-born happiness."
But the corpse knew death was far better
than poverty and remains silent.

ON A RAINY DAY

Fortunate is the lover who helps his mistress
to change clothes when she comes over on a rainy day.
The kohl around her eyes is washed off by the rain,
and her sheer blue cloth, clinging to her shapely breasts,
reveals the natural beauty of her figure.

WHEN WINTER COMES

The rich are excited by the coming of winter:
with mouths full of fresh betel nut,
their bodies feast on endless joys
as they lie fondling their dark women.
But we who are poor are desperate—
our laps, barely covered by worn-out rags—
collect no bounty but the quaking of our knees.

JEWELS

The cloth around her hips slipped
as the fire of love ran its course.
The warm vibrant jewels of her girdle
seemed to drape her in a rustle of silk.
While her lover despaired of ever seeing her
in all her glory, the lovely girl blushed
in vain with embarrassment.
But when he tried to pull her veil off,
she stopped him, although she didn't
quite manage to hide her nakedness.

THE CREAKING BED

The night was far gone;
the lamp burned with a steady flame.
But my lover knew a thing or two
about the rites of passion.
He made love slowly, cautiously,
was forced to hold back his body
as the bed creaked like an enemy,
grinding his teeth in rage.

SHE PROTESTS TOO MUCH

"Girl, you be the lover, I'll be the loved one."
"No, never," she protested, shaking her head.
But she let the bracelet slip from her wrist
to mine and gave in without a word.

SHE DOESN'T LET GO OF HER PRIDE

She turns aside his eyes,
riveted on her breasts,
by embracing him.
She puts rouge on her lips,
seeing his lips burn for hers.
She stops his hand on her crotch
by closing her thighs tight.
Tactfully, she neither rejects
her husband's love
nor lets go of her pride.

THE WAYS OF LOVE

With a curse, the woman threw her lover out,
despite his groveling at her feet.
But when he began to walk out of the room,
she ran to stop him, with head bowed
and the knot of her skirt in her palms.
Strange are the ways of love.

A LOVER'S WORD

No, my husband isn't stupid.
Though the moon is shining and the way rough,
and everyone's fond of gossip,
a lover's word may not be broken.
So with love on her mind, a certain girl
sets out to keep her tryst:
many times she leaves her house,
and as many times she returns.

THE HAWK

Undisturbed a hawk circles freely high above
till he hangs perfectly still in midair.
Looking down, he spies a chunk of meat
cooking in the backyard of an outcaste's hut.
He draws in the full span of his moving wings
for the swift descent, and in an instant snatches
the half-cooked meat from the pot.

A NEEDLE

Worn down by hunger, the children are like corpses;
relatives have forsaken me;
the broken water pot is glued with lac.
But none of this hurts me more
than our neighbor sneering at my wife,
annoyed that she asks every day
to borrow a needle to darn her ragged clothes.

TIME WASTED

I wear no bracelet,
clear as the rays of the autumn moon.
I haven't drunk from the lips
of a shy, tender bride,
nor have I won, by sword or pen,
fame in Indra's world.
Instead I've wasted my time
in ramshackle schools,
teaching impudent, spiteful students.

THE SCHOLAR'S LIFE

Just as she blossoms into a charming woman,
you leave behind your young wife
and become a student who lives off charity
and sleeps alone for many years.
Though you've gained knowledge,
you're worn out with the endless wandering.
The scholar's life be damned!
The reward it brings isn't worth
the pleasure or the pain.

FOOLISH HEART

A cheerless wife, relatives struck by misfortune,
friends turned into strangers,
servants reduced to poverty,
an uneasy mind, and a hardscrabble life—
such are the blows fate deals a man.
Yet his foolish heart yearns for happiness.

SUPREME BLISS

The sky, my cloth; the hollow of my hand, my bowl;
deer, my companions; meditation, my sleep;
the earth, my bed; roots, my food.
When will I have what I long for with all my heart—
the noble, supreme bliss?

BĀṆA

IN A CORNER OF THE VILLAGE SHRINE

At dusk, the traveler huddles near a bonfire,
perfectly content and unmindful of his singed clothes.
Later, he falls asleep on a bed of straw
in the shrine of the village goddess,
only to be woken up by a gust of frosty wind.
His threadbare scruffy garment is cold:
shivering and groaning,
he scurries from one corner into another.

BHARTṚHARI

WISE MEN

In this shallow fickle world,
wise men choose two courses:
for a time they keep the company of minds
steeped in the ocean of wisdom.
They spend the rest with nubile young women
whose full hips and breasts
glow with the pleasure of hiding
men's impatient hands
in the depths of their thighs.

POETS' EXCESSES

Surely her face is not the full moon,
her eyes are not a pair of blue lotuses,
nor is her soft body made of gold.
Yet deceived by poets' excesses,
a foolish man, despite knowing the truth,
will worship a woman's body
that is no more than skin, flesh, and bones.

THE LOVE GAME

At first she pleads with me,
"No, not now, please."
But soon the petting and fondling
light the fire of passion in her.
Almost unnoticed, her limbs relax;
resolve ebbs away.
Hot with desire, she brazenly
throws herself into the love game
and spreads her legs out
in an arc of never-ending pleasure.
Such are the joys
when a man makes love to his wife.

HIPS

With words of eloquent wisdom
learned men talk of renouncing all worldly ties.
But who can honestly turn away
from beautiful women's hips
girdled with strands of rubies?

FEAR OF DEATH

The craving for pleasure is gone,
the respect of men is lost,
friends and peers have moved on to heaven,
one depends on a cane just to get around,
the eyes are shrouded in darkness—
yet this foolish body is terrified of death.

DESIRE ALONE

My face is lined with wrinkles,
my hair has turned gray,
my limbs have become feeble.
Desire alone stays forever young.

ADORATION OF WOMAN

Those lumps of flesh, her breasts,
are compared to golden bowls.
That storehouse of phlegm, her face,
is compared to the moon.
Damp with urine, her thigh
is said to surpass the elephant's trunk.
Look, how poets embellish her vile body.

THE POET SPEAKS TO THE KING

You are a lord of riches; words obey my call.
You are a man of arms;
my undying eloquence vanquishes pride.
Those blinded by wealth slave for you,
but they are eager to hear me
to rid their minds of evil.
Since you have no respect for me, king,
I respect you even less. I shall leave.

CONTENTMENT

The earth, his bed;
limbs of creepers, his pillow;
the sky, the roof over his head;
pleasant winds, his fan;
the bright moon, his lamp;
attachment to Lady Indifference, his joy.
Calm, smeared with ash,
the hermit sleeps in comfort
like a king.

MAN'S LIFE

Man's life span is a hundred years:
half of it is spent in sleep; of the rest,
youth and old age take up another half.
He spends much of what's left toiling for others,
dogged by sickness, pain, and separation.
In this life, unstable as the waves of the sea,
where can man find happiness?

OLD AGE

Your body shrinks, steps falter, teeth fall out,
eyes dim, ears fail, you drool at the mouth.
Relatives ignore your words, the wife doesn't care,
your son has only contempt for you.
O the wretchedness of man in old age!

WHITE FLAG

The moment young women notice
the hair on a man's head has turned white—
the flag of his surrender to old age—
they avoid him from afar
as they would the outcastes' well,
branded with a pile of bones.

BHĀSKARA II

ELEMENTARY ARITHMETIC

A woman's necklace of pearls broke while making love.
A third of the pearls rolled onto the floor,
one-fifth was scattered on the bed,
she herself retrieved one-sixth,
and her lover picked up one-tenth.
If only six pearls remained on the string,
how many pearls did the necklace have?

BHAVABHŪTI

THE CRITIC SCORNED

Those who have contempt for my work
are free to think as they please.
What I write is not for their ears
but for one who will be born someday
with a temperament like mine.
For time is infinite and the earth, boundless.

BHĀVAKADEVĪ

BITTER HARVEST

How our bodies were as one before.
Then you stopped being the lover,
but I, wretched one, kept on playing the beloved.
Now you're the husband, and I'm the wife.
What is left but to reap the fruit
of my diamond-hard life?

BHOJA

SCRAMBLING OUT OF THE WATER

She shakes off the fresh drops of water
from the tips of her unkempt hair
and crosses her arms to hide
the strain of her growing breasts;
a silk cloth clings tight to her shapely thighs.
She bends down a little, scans the riverbank,
and scrambles out of the water in no time.

BILHAṆA

BITE MARKS

I still remember her coy sidelong looks
as her body moved in a fever of love,
showing the curve of her shapely breast
as the hem of her cloth slipped,
and her lip flaunted the marks of my teeth.

IN LIFE AFTER LIFE

I still remember her eyes,
flickering, closed after making love,
her supple body relaxed,
clothes and hair in disarray:
a wild goose caught in the lotus thickets of love.
I shall remember her in death,
even in life after life.

ALL FOR LOVE

If I could still see her at day's end,
my fawn-eyed woman who revives me
with her breasts, pots filled with nectar,
kingly pleasures, sweet heaven itself,
even my salvation I would forgo.

DEVAGUPTA

DRUMBEATS

Silly girl, you go to meet your lover
with a string of pearls bouncing on your breasts,
a girdle clanking on your hips,
and jeweled anklets tinkling on your feet.
Yet, with such telltale drumbeats,
you are panic-stricken,
looking furtively in every direction.

DHARMAKĪRTI

THE WAY

No one walks ahead; no one follows behind.
On this path, no new footprints;
a wilderness now where the ancients walked.
The other path is broad and pleasant,
but I have turned my back on it.
Alone now, I know the way.

JAGANNĀTHA PAṆḌITARĀJA

INDRA'S HEAVEN

If I could get her to sleep with me just once—
the Muslim girl with an ever-so-soft body—
(even if the bed is a bare mud floor),
all the pleasures of Indra's heaven I'd spurn.

JAGHANACAPALĀ

WIFE

Nothing turns on a hot-assed woman more
than the wind howling on a rainy night
in empty streets, and a husband who's away.

KĀLIDĀSA

FLIGHT OF THE DEER

Time and again he looks back,
his neck turned gracefully,
at the speeding chariot that pursues him.
Terrified of the falling arrow,
his haunches close in on his chest:
panting at the mouth, he leaves a trail
of half-chewed grass on the path.
Look how he flies through the air
almost in defiance of the earth!

SUCH INNOCENT MOVES

The moment my fingers touch her girdle,
trembling she stays my roaming hand;
as soon as I press her close to my chest,
she defends her breasts with her arms;
when I gaze at her lash-wide look,
she quickly turns aside her face.
With such innocent moves she grants my heart's desires.

BLESSED SLEEP

Take pity on me, blessed Sleep.
I beg of you to show me once more
my dear girl for just a moment.
When she appears, I shall lock her in my arms
so she cannot leave.
But if she leaves, I too shall leave with her.

KARṆOTPALA

THE LAMP

When I undid her silk blouse,
she crossed her arms at once over her breasts.
When I unwrapped the skirt from her hips,
she closed her thighs tight.
She nearly died of embarrassment
when my eyes fastened onto her secret places.
She then hurled at the lamp the lotus from her ear
and put out the quivering flame.

KEŚAṬA

THE CAMEL

He is back from his travels in the endless desert,
and his wife can't take her eyes off him
as they brim with tears of joy.
She spoils his camel with palm and thornleaf
and wipes the thick layer of dust from its mane
gently with the hem of her skirt.

KṢEMENDRA

ALL EYES ON THE DOOR

Once her lover departed, the bed vanished from the house;
the garlands of stale flowers were tossed out.
With daybreak came her doting former lover
whom she had stood up that night.
As he began to undo the knot of her skirt,
she kicked him in the leg and complained,
"I slept all alone, my eyes glued to the door!"
With that the courtesan chased away his blues.

KṢITĪŚA

THE RED SEAL

When will I see her generous thighs again,
shut tight at first out of modesty,
then opening surprised by desire,
revealing, as her silk wrap comes loose,
the fine purple marks of my fingernails
like a red seal inscribed on a treasure?

KUMĀRADĀSA

ALBA

Come now, unwind yourself
from the arms of your lover;
yet how coy you were at the first meeting.
The sun has cast its rays here,
and the roosters have begun to crow.

KUṬALĀ

FURTIVE LOVEMAKING

Nothing compares, even remotely—
not the pleasures of betel leaves
or of hugging and kissing in bed—
with brief, hurried, furtive lovemaking.

MĀGHA

THE ART OF POETRY

Did grammar ever feed the hungry?
Did the nectar of poetry ever quench anyone's thirst?
No one can raise a family on book learning.
Make your pile and screw the arts.

SCENT

You can hide her fingernail marks with your shawl,
hide with your hand the lip she has bitten,
but can you hide her scent that blows
in every direction, shouting out your adultery?

MAHODADHI

STOP BEING WILLFUL

The night is almost over, love,
and the moon has all but vanished.
Overcome by sleep, the lamp flickers.
A woman should stop being willful
once a man grants her wishes;
yet you haven't let go of your anger.
Being so close to your firm breasts,
even your heart's grown hard.

MORIKĀ

DON'T GO

A hundred times I've told you gently,
"Don't go; my mistress loves you so."
When you step into the courtyard to leave,
your young wife is heartbroken.
What more can I say? Her firmly tied bodice,
that bears the weight of her breasts,
rips at the seams, and I have used up every bit
of thread in the house, sewing it day in, day out.

MURĀRI

HIDDEN FINGERNAIL MARKS

In the morning when friends press her
for details of the night's intimacies,
the bride lowers her head in shame.
But when they embellish her breasts with musk
and sandalwood paste, her body shudders
and reveals the hidden fingernail marks.

AN ACTOR IN A FARCE

Feeble of voice and body,
toadying to the rich and powerful,
I've become an actor in a farce.
I have no clue in what low comedy
old age expects me to dance
with these pathetic gray hairs for makeup.

RĀJAPUTRA PARPAṬI

BLOW OUT THE LAMP

"Wait a moment; let go of my skirt.
You'll wake up the servants.
Shame on you! With folded hands
I beg of you to blow out the lamp."
My beloved's words delight me
more than even making love.

RĀJAŚEKHARA

HER FACE

Blot out the dark night with brushes heavy with ink;
wipe off the lily's smile with spells;
lay the moon on a flat stone and crush it to pieces
that I may see the whole earth engraved with her face.

RUDRAṬA

WHAT THE YOUNG WIFE SAID TO THE TRAVELER

My aged mother sleeps here, and over there
my father, one of the oldest of men;
here, worn out with toil, sleeps the slave girl;
and here I sleep alone, unfortunate me,
for my husband's been gone for some days.
With such beguiling words, the young wife
conveyed what's on her mind to the traveler.

ŚARAṆA

GIRL DRAWING WATER FROM A WELL

As she lifts her slender arm to pull on the rope,
her breast shows on that side;
her conch-shell bangles shake and clink,
almost snapping the thread.
With her generous thighs spread apart
and her shapely buttocks thrust out as she bends,
the outcaste girl draws water again and again from the well.

SIDDHOKA

THE EMPTY ROAD

The day was almost over; darkness had fallen.
The traveler's wife had scanned the empty road
far and wide for her husband.
With a heavy heart, she walks toward
their whitewashed house; but thinking,
"Perhaps he may come now," looks back once more.

ŚĪLĀBHAṬṬĀRIKĀ

THEN AND NOW

My husband is the same man who stole my virginity.
These are the same moonlit nights;
the same breeze floats down from the Vindhya mountains,
thick with the scent of flowering jasmine.
I too am the same woman. Yet I long with all my heart
for the thicket of reeds by the river
that once knew our wild joyous lovemaking.

SONNOKA

DRIVEN BY PASSION

Fortunate is the man whose woman,
driven by passion, pleasures him
by switching roles in lovemaking.
Her moaning blends with her tinkling waist bells
that swing as she moves her hips.
Her hair comes undone, the pearl necklace snaps,
and her breasts heave with every breath.

ŚRĪHARṢA

THE SMART GIRL

To avoid sitting close together,
she rises to welcome him from afar.
To ward off his embraces,
she busies herself with folding betel leaves.
To prevent any talk between them,
she bosses the servants around.
With such gestures, the smart girl tactfully
deflects her anger toward her husband.

IN HER DIRECTION

Between him and the woman he loves
yawn a hundred lands, rivers, forests, mountains;
try as he might, there's no way he can see her.
Yet, eyes hot with tears,
the traveler stands on tiptoe, craning his neck,
and for a long time looks wistfully in her direction.

VALLAṆA

SEA OF SHAME

Once he had peeled my clothes off,
my arms could not hide my breasts;
his chest became my only covering.
When his hand plunged below my hips,
who could have saved me, drowning in a sea of shame,
but the god of love himself
who teaches us how to faint?

ON THE GRASS

Having thrown your shawl on the grass
by the pond, traveler, you sit on it.
Aren't you tired? The way is difficult,
with no village in sight; besides, it's getting late.
No longer covered by the shawl, your thighs show
as you raise your knees to your stomach.
It is twice as unseemly as if you were sprawled out.
I too am alone. What are we to make of this?

THE ESSENCE OF POETRY

The essence of poetry
is not in what the words say
but in how they say it.
This and not some special flavor
gives pleasure.

Not naked
but glimpsed in a flash
through silk ruffled by a breeze
does a woman's breast
give pleasure.

VARĀHA

PORING OVER A BOOK

At times he opens his eyes wide,
rubs them with his hands and peers intently,
looks at it from afar or moves it closer,
or steps out into the light to see better
but remembers the eye ointment he's left behind.
So does a man in old age pore over a book.

VIDYĀ

HOLLOW PLEASURES

If just looking at the woman is not enough
to make her lover come, and if he still continues
to embrace her, the pleasure she offers him is hollow.
But if after being loved, she pursues another lover,
she is no better than a tramp and is beneath contempt.
Why, even birds and beasts have their fill of love
once they have huddled close to each other's flanks.

COMPLAINT

How fortunate you are, my friends!
You can speak openly about the goings-on
with your lovers: the idle talk, the laughter
and fun, the endless rounds of pleasure.
As for me, once my lover undid the knot of my skirt,
I swear, I remember nothing.

THE RIVERBANK

He can't stand well water, the child's father,
refuses to touch it. Would you, neighbor,
keep an eye on the house for a moment
while I slip out, though I'm alone, to the riverbank,
overhung with gamboge and spiked with reeds
whose broken shoots may scrape against my breasts?

VIKAṬANITAMBĀ

THE BED

As he approached the bed, the knot gave way on its own;
the skirt clung to my hips, held somehow
by only the cords of the unsteady belt.
That's all I know, dear friend.
But once he took me in his arms, I don't remember
who he was, who I was, or what we did.

A WORD OF ADVICE

Stop fretting about the girl being young and fragile.
Whoever has seen a mango blossom
snap from the weight of a bee?
Throw caution to the wind:
squeeze her hard when the two of you are alone.
Sugarcane, pressed gently, will not release its juice.

YOGEŚVARA

FAR FROM HOME

A cool breeze blows after the heavy downpour;
the sky is awash with clouds;
a flash of lightning reveals all of space in an instant;
the moon, stars, planets are fast asleep;
the keen scent of rain-drenched kadamba blossoms drifts in;
a chorus of frogs overwhelms the darkness.
How does a lover, far from home, get through such nights?

WHEN THE RAINS COME

The river overflowing its banks fills my heart with delight:
on top of a canebrake, a snake is asleep;
a moorhen calls out; geese clamor;
herds of deer gather in knots;
the thick grass is weighed down by streams of ants;
and the jungle fowl is drunk with joy.

NOTES

I have followed Siegfried Lienhard, *A History of Classical Poetry: Sanskrit, Pāli, Prākrit* (Wiesbaden: Harrassowitz, 1984), for information on the poets. All line references are to the English texts. The translations are my own unless otherwise noted.

THAT'S HOW I SAW HER

Abhinanda (ca. 850–900) was a poet from Bengal.

4: The *Kāmasūtra* (2.4.1–31) describes the practice of scratching with the fingernails and lists eight kinds of marks: the knife stroke, the half-moon, the circle, the line, the tiger's claw, the peacock's foot, the hare's leap, and the leaf of a blue lotus. The peacock's foot, for example, is described as marks made on the breast by pulling the nipple with all five fingernails.

In the excitement of passion, the lovers left the marks of their fingernails on each other's bodies. Fingernail marks are a prelude to lovemaking and are therefore treasured as souvenirs. As Vātsyāyana informs us (2.4.28):

> If there are no fingernail marks to evoke
> memories of the seats of passion,

then passion has long since waned
and love itself has vanished.

The Belgian poet Nicole Houssa (1930–1959) echoes Vātsyāyana's statement in "Star":

And I for my part
Have pinned on your breast
Ten stars in the form of nail marks
So that you do not forget me.

(Evelyne Sullerot, *Women on Love: Eight Centuries of Feminine Writing*, trans. Helen R. Lane [Garden City, N.Y.: Doubleday, 1979], 264)

WHO NEEDS THE GODS?

Amaru or Amarūka (7th cent.) was the compiler of *Amaru's One Hundred Poems*. For a reading of the poem, see the introduction, pp. xxviii–xxix. Compare with Bilhaṇa's "All for Love" (p. 61).

A TASTE OF AMBROSIA

1: The *Kāmasūtra* (2.4.1–31 and 2.5.1–43) recommends scratching and biting to arouse sexual desire. "Every part of the body can be bitten, except the upper lip, the tongue, and the eyes" (2.5.1). There are eight kinds of love bites: the hidden, the swollen, the point, the row of points, coral and jewel, the row of gems, the scattered cloud, and the boar's bite. The first three bites are made on the lower lip (2.5.4). The scattered cloud, for example, is described as a circle of irregular tooth marks below the breast.

8–9: In the beginning, the gods and demons churned the ocean to obtain the nectar of immortality. The gods obtained it with the help of Viṣṇu, the Supreme Being. Amaru subverts the myth to imply that the man found nectar the instant he kissed the woman's lips; he did not have to churn the ocean like the foolish gods.

THE BRIDE

2: It was customary to keep an oil lamp burning during lovemaking.

THE PLEDGE

For a reading of the poem, see the introduction, pp. xxvi–xxvii.

STONEHEARTED

4: Moonstones are believed to ooze drops of water when touched by the moon's rays.

WALKING THE STREET BY HER HOUSE

6: The motif of walking the street of the beloved is common in poetry. If such an ordinary act could send the lover into raptures, what effect would the consummation of his love have on him? Compare with the following lines from the poem "Nannina" by the Italian poet Salvatore Di Giacomo (1860–1934):

> Three days I wearily walked the pavement,
> watching for the covert eyes of my joy;
> not a sound, the shutter was bolted fast,
> only a dim light on that balcony.
>
> (Salvatore Di Giacomo, *Love Poems: A Selection*, trans. Frank J. Palescandolo, Essential Poets 79 [Toronto: Guernica, 1999], 11).

THE SHEETS

For a reading of the poem, see the introduction, pp. xix–xxiii.

AUBADE

After a night of wild lovemaking, the woman betrays what William Blake (1757–1827) calls the lineaments of gratified desire.

LIKE THE WHEELS OF A CHARIOT

Yama and his sister, Yamī, were the first mortals. When they died, they went to the underworld, over which Yama presided as the god of death. Yama rejects his sister's overtures. The poem is remarkable for its conflation of the erotic and the heroic.

THE WORD

The word does not reveal itself to the uninitiated; only the initiated know the word. It is somewhat unusual to speak of the revelation of the word in erotic terms.

AN INVITATION

3: The field, like the plow, is a fertility symbol. The plow working the field represents man fertilizing woman. The field could therefore mean the womb. For a note on "traveler" poems, see the introduction, pp. xxxi–xxxiii.

HAIR

The poem can be read in two different ways, either as an erotic poem or as a poem about asceticism. It involves the use of the rhetorical figure of implied metaphor (*samāsokti*), which the critic Udbhaṭa (8th–9th cent.) defines as follows: "When a theme, other than the original one, is made known in a sentence through common attributes, it is said to be *samāsokti*"

(*Kāvyālaṃkārasārasaṃgraḥ* of Udbhaṭa, ed., with the commentary the *Laghuvṛtti* of Indurāja, by Narayana Daso Banhatti, Bombay Sanskrit and Prākrit Series, no. 79, 2nd ed. [Poona: Bhandarkar Oriental Research Institute, 1982], 41). Udbhaṭa offers the following example (42):

With flowers that are her shining teeth,
with sprouts that are her hands,
the lovely woman approaches the water,
her hair knotted like a cluster of bees.

The commentary identifies the "original theme" as Pārvatī, spouse of Śiva. The attributes (flowers, sprouts, and bees) apply equally to the vine, the "secondary theme," which is only implied; *vana* is both "water" and "woods" in Sanskrit. While one theme ("lovely woman") is explicitly stated, another ("the vine") is implied. The poem "Hair" can also be translated as follows:

Having renounced the close bonds of affection,
the genial clean-shaven hermits inhale smoke
as they set out on the path of liberation.
But they are in shackles again as they linger
on the world's shore. It is difficult indeed
to break away from all worldly ties.

In Udbhaṭa's example, only *vana* is a pun; but our poem bristles with puns: *snehaṃ* (semen; affection), *dhūman* (perfume; smoke), *mokṣapathaṃ* (untied; path of liberation), *nitamba* (loins; shore). The vocabulary of Sanskrit, unlike that of most languages, is unusually polysemic.

THANK OFFERING

4: Funeral rites include the offering of cooked rice, sesame, and water to the dead, who are placed on a bed of kusa grass (*Poa cynosuroides* Retz).

Pubic hair is considered unclean, so women remove it periodically. That this practice has been around for centuries is borne out by the sculptures of women with clean-shaved vulvas in the temples of Khajuraho (10th–11th cent.) in Madhya Pradesh. Greek women, too, as Aristophanes's (ca. 445–ca. 385 B.C.E.) plays indicate, shaved their pubic hair but only partially. They shaped the hair to draw attention to their vulvas and thereby make themselves sexually more attractive. The methods used for depilation included plucking and singeing by lamp. The German ethnographer Hermann Heinrich Ploss (1819–1885) reported that in India "rings of a special shape are used for the purpose of depilation and to this end are worn on the thumb. They resemble unusually large signet rings with flat, sharp-edged discs set with tiny mirrors, which both show the areas in question and reflect the light. The shaving is done with the sharp edges. The name for these rings is *ārsī*" (Hermann Heinrich Ploss, Max Bartels, and Paul Bartels, *Woman: An Historical, Gynaecological, and Anthropological Compendium*, ed. Eric John Dingwall, 3 vols. [London: Heinemann, 1935], 1:377).

WHEN WINTER COMES

2: Betel nut is generally chewed with betel leaf and mineral lime as a stimulant and to freshen the mouth.

THE CREAKING BED

7: The motif of the creaking bed (*argutatio lecti*) is a familiar one in poetry. Here the bed has the upper hand; it dictates how the lovers make love. Feeble and run down, it creaks loudly as it can no longer withstand the vigorous lovemaking.

Catullus's (ca. 84–54 B.C.E.) "Poem 6" is a fine example of the motif in Latin.

> Look at your bed
> still trembling with your labours
> (tell me that you sleep alone)
> sheets soiled with love and flowers . . .

(Catullus, *The Poems of Catullus*, trans. Horace Gregory [New York: Grove Press, 1956], 12).

THE WAYS OF LOVE

5: It is as though the woman is handing over the "knot of her skirt" to the man to do with her as he pleases. After the initial defiance, she surrenders herself to him completely.

A LOVER'S WORD

See the reading of the poem "On a Rainy Day" in the introduction, pp. xxix–xxxi.

THE HAWK

4: "Outcaste" is the translation of *caṇḍāla*. The *caṇḍāla*s are the offspring of mixed marriages between Shudra men and Brahman women. Today they would be termed Dalits, "oppressed, downtrodden." The *caṇḍāla* tends the cremation ground. He is socially defenseless; in the poem, even the hawk gets the better of him.

TIME WASTED

6: Indra is the king of the gods; his world is heaven. Unsuccessful in his search for a patron, the poet gives vent to his frustrations.

THE SCHOLAR'S LIFE

Compare with the following lines from W. B. Yeats's (1865–1939) poem "The Scholars" (1919):

> Old, learned, respectable bald heads
> Edit and annotate the lines

That young men, tossing on their beds,
Rhymed out in love's despair.

(W. B. Yeats, *The Collected Works of W. B. Yeats, Volume 1: The Poems*, ed. Richard J. Finneran, rev. ed. [New York: Macmillan, 1989], 140–41).

See also Māgha's poem "The Art of Poetry" (p. 75).

SUPREME BLISS

5: "Supreme bliss" is the translation of *paramapāritoṣa*. Having renounced the world and become a hermit, the speaker only wishes for liberation from the endless cycle of birth, death, and rebirth.

IN A CORNER OF THE VILLAGE SHRINE

Bāṇa (7th cent.) was a poet at the court of King Harṣa (r. 606–647) in Kānyakubja (present-day Kannauj in Uttar Pradesh) and is best known for his prose romance *Kādambarī*.

1: "Bonfire" is the translation of *puṇyāgni*. A large fire was usually built in the open air in a village for the benefit of travelers. The fire's sponsor would acquire merit for his good works.

WISE MEN

Nothing is known of Bhartṛhari (ca. 400). For a reading of the poem, see the introduction, xxxvi–xxxvii.

POETS' EXCESSES

5–6: Philosophical poet that he was, Bhartṛhari was both fascinated by woman's body and repelled by it. This is a recurring theme in his poetry. Compare with "Adoration of Woman" (p. 49).

THE LOVE GAME

3–4: The *Kāmasūtra* (2.2.1–31) notes that a woman's desire is aroused when a man pets and fondles her. The god of love Kāma's five arrows target five parts of a woman's body: heart, breasts, eyes, forehead, and vulva. The arrows are tipped with the red lotus, asoka, mango, jasmine, and blue lotus flowers.

HIPS

Compare with these lines from Lucille Clifton's (1936–2010) poem "homage to my hips" (1980):

> i have known them
> to put a spell on a man and
> spin him like a top!
>
> (Lucille Clifton, *The Collected Poems of Lucille Clifton, 1965–2010*, ed. Kevin Young and Michael S. Glaser [Rochester, N.Y.: BOA Editions, 2012], 198).

ADORATION OF WOMAN

Bhartṛhari calls into question, as Shakespeare does in Sonnet 130, the conventional representations of the beloved. The hyperboles in both poems are of course ironic.

> My mistress' eyes are nothing like the sun;
> Coral is far more red than her lips' red;
> . . .
> And in some perfumes is there more delight
> Than in the breath that from my mistress reeks.
>
> (Katherine Duncan-Jones, ed., *Shakespeare's Sonnets*, The Arden Shakespeare [London: Nelson, 1997], 375).

THE POET SPEAKS TO THE KING

For a reading of the poem, see the introduction, pp. xliii–xliv. Other poets, such as Horace (65–8 B.C.E.) and Ovid (43 B.C.E.–?17 C.E.), have made similar claims for their "pow'rful rhyme." Here are the closing lines of the latter's *Metamorphoses*, Book 15:

> As long as Rome is the Eternal City
> These lines shall echo from the lips of men,
> As long as poetry speaks truth on earth,
> That immortality is mine to wear.
> (Ovid, *The Metamorphoses*, trans. Horace Gregory [New York: Viking, 1958], 441).

WHITE FLAG

Nowhere is Bhartṛhari more cynical than in this poem, which is awash with taedium vitae.

5–6: A cluster of bones is hung on top of a well to warn everyone that the well is only for the use of outcastes.

ELEMENTARY ARITHMETIC

Bhāskara II (1114–1185), along with Āryabhaṭa (476–550) and Brahmagupta (598–668), laid the foundations of Indian mathematics. He was the head of an astronomical observatory in Ujjayinī (present-day Ujjain in Madhya Pradesh). The poem appears in Ramakrishna Deva's *Manorañjana* (Entertainment), a commentary on Bhāskara II's treatise on arithmetic, *Līlāvatī* (The beautiful). It is quoted in Henry Thomas Colebrooke's (1765–1837) translation of the *Līlāvatī* (1817) in a footnote to verse 54. There were in all thirty pearls in the necklace.

THE CRITIC SCORNED

Bhavabhūti (8th cent.) was a poet at the court of King Yaśovarman of Kānyakubja. Of the three surviving plays by him, *The Later Story of Rama* (*Uttararāmacarita*) is one of the finest achievements of Sanskrit drama. This well-known verse appears in the play *Mālatī and Mādhava* (*Mālatīmādhava*, 1.6).

3–5: The Urdu poet Mirza Ghalib (1797–1869) famously expressed a similar hope in Persian:

> Today none buys my verse's wine, that it may grow in age
> To make the senses reel in many a drinker yet to come.
> My star rose highest in the firmament before my birth;
> My poetry will win the world's acclaim when I am gone.

(Ralph Russell, ed., *The Oxford India Ghalib: Life, Letters and Ghazals* [New Delhi: Oxford University Press, 2003], 518).

BITTER HARVEST

Bhāvakadevī was a woman poet.

5–6: Compared with the time when they were lovers, marriage seems to have taken the romance out of their lives. It is this unhappy realization that she finds hard to accept. Compare with Śīlābhaṭṭārikā's poem "Then and Now" (p. 86) on the same theme.

SCRAMBLING OUT OF THE WATER

Bhoja (11th cent.) was the king of Dhārā in present-day Madhya Pradesh. He is best known for a work on poetics, *Light on Love* (*Śṛṅgāraprakāśa*).

BITE MARKS

Bilhaṇa (11th cent.) is the author of a poetic sequence titled *Fifty Poems of a Thief of Love* (*Caurapañcāśikā*). See p. xviii on Bilhaṇa's travails in finding a patron.

5: For "marks of my teeth," see note (p. 102) on "A Taste of Ambrosia."

DRUMBEATS

A Telugu poem, "Tryst" (Abhisārika), by Duvvuri Ramireddy (1895–1947), echoes Devagupta's poem.

In the middle of the night
you go to meet your lover,
softly,
as if walking on air.

You hold your anklets in your hand
so they don't make a sound.

When the owl hoots from his midnight nest,
you look over your shoulder, scared.

You are startled at your own footsteps,
and cry, "Who's that?"

In your white dress
and your light skin,
no one can see you
in the flood of moonlight.

But the fragrance of your body—
it spreads where you walk.

Girl,
how do you disguise that?

(Velcheru Narayana Rao, ed. and trans., *Hibiscus on the Lake: Twentieth-Century Telugu Poetry from India* [Madison: University of Wisconsin Press, 2003], 46).

THE WAY

Dharmakīrti (7th cent.), a Brahman from present-day Tamil Nadu, was a Buddhist philosopher who wrote a number of influential works on logic. The poem describes well the poet's discovery of new thresholds away from the beaten path.

INDRA'S HEAVEN

Jagannātha Paṇḍitarāja (17th cent.), a Telugu Brahman from present-day Andhra Pradesh, wrote the last great work on Sanskrit poetics, the *Rasagaṅgādhara* (The Ganges bearer [Śiva] of mood). At the Mughal court of Shāh Jahān (r. 1628–1658), Jagannātha is said to have fallen in love with a Muslim girl whom he later married. We know her only as Lavaṅgī, and seven verses in praise of her beauty are attributed to the poet. The story is retold in a Tamil movie, *Lavaṅkī* (1946), directed by Y. V. Rao, and in a Marathi play, *Paṇḍitrāj Jagannāth* (1960), written by Vidyadhar Gokhale and produced by Bhalchandra Pendharkar.

I have translated *navanītakomalāṅgī* (literally, "girl with a body soft as butter") as "girl with an ever-so-soft body." The comparison of a girl's body to freshly churned butter does not sit well in English. It has been suggested by Aryendra Sharma that the phrase *navanītakomalāṅgī* may well be a translation of the Hindi phrase *makkhan ki putlī* (a lovely woman [soft as] butter). Jagannātha was, no doubt, familiar with the conventions of Hindi and Urdu poetry of his time. He attempted to breathe life into Sanskrit poetry by introducing new images.

FLIGHT OF THE DEER

Kālidāsa (4th–5th cent.), the preeminent poet in Sanskrit, was the author of three long poems, *The Cloud Messenger* (*Meghadūta*), *The Origin of the Young God* (*Kumārasaṃbhava*), and *The Dynasty of Raghu* (*Raghuvaṃśa*), and of three plays, including his masterpiece, *Śakuntalā and the Ring of Recollection* (*Abhijñānaśākuntala*), where this well-known verse appears (1.7).

SUCH INNOCENT MOVES

This verse appears in Kalidasa's play *Mālavikā and Agnimitra* (*Mālavikāgnimitra*, 4.15).

THE LAMP

6: "Secret places" is the translation of *nābhimūla* (the part of the body below the navel).

7–8: The motif of the flickering lamp in the lovers' bedroom is a familiar one in poetry.

THE CAMEL

Keśaṭa is praised by Yogeśvara in VSR 1733.

4–6: Social conventions do not allow a wife to show affection to her husband in public. Besides, her in-laws might be present. She therefore expresses her joy on seeing him on his return from a journey by treating his camel kindly, by feeding it and wiping the dust off its mane.

ALL EYES ON THE DOOR

Kṣemendra (11th cent.) was a prolific poet and critic from Kashmir whose patrons were King Ananta (r. 1029–1064) and his son, King Kalasa

(r. 1064–1088) of Kashmir. His *Critical Discourse on Propriety* (*Aucityavicāracarcā*) is a landmark in Sanskrit poetics.

THE RED SEAL

Nothing is known of Kṣitīśa.

5: For fingernail marks, see note (pp. 101–102) on "That's How I Saw Her."

6: The "red seal" refers to his fingernail marks, and the "treasure" is the woman's vulva, the ultimate object of the man's desire.

ALBA

Kumāradāsa (7th–8th cent.) was the author of a long poem, *The Abduction of Sita* (*Jānakīharaṇa*). The poem is an example of the dawn song, or alba, in Sanskrit poetry. The alba is a lament over the parting of lovers at daybreak. The woman's girlfriend warns her of the arrival of dawn with the crowing of the rooster. The lovers must now part. The poem also features the motif of stolen love. The alba appeared in Tamil earlier than it did in Sanskrit. Here is a Tamil example, "The Cockcrow," by Allūr Naṉmullaiyār (1st–3rd cent.):

> The minute the cock sounded *co-coo*,
> panic seized my innocent heart.
> Daylight fell upon us—
> a sword that tore me apart
> from my lover entangled in my arms.

(*Kuṟuntokai* [An anthology of short poems], comp. Pūrikkō, ed. U. Ve. Caminataiyar [Annamalai Nagar: Annamalai University, 1983], 309).

FURTIVE LOVEMAKING

Kuṭalā was a woman poet. This is her only poem that has survived.

2: For "betel leaves," see note (p. 106) on "When Winter Comes."

4: The locus classicus of the motif of stolen love is Śīlābhaṭṭārikā's poem "Then and Now" (p. 86).

THE ART OF POETRY

Māgha (7th cent.) is best known for his long poem *The Slaying of Śiśupāla* (*Śiśupālavadha*). Compare with the following lines from the Russian poet Vladimir Mayakovsky's (1893–1930) poem "At the Top of My Voice" (1930):

My verse
has brought me
no roubles to spare:
no craftsmen have made
mahogany chairs for my house.

(Yevgeny Yevtushenko, comp., *Twentieth-Century Russian Poetry: Silver and Steel; An Anthology*, ed. Albert C. Todd and Max Hayward [New York: Doubleday, 1993], 272).

SCENT

1: For "fingernail marks," see note (pp. 101–102) on "That's How I Saw Her."

2: For "the lip she has bitten," see note (p. 102) on "A Taste of Ambrosia."

The husband returns home at dawn to his wife, bearing the marks of his infidelity. He had probably spent the night with a courtesan.

Scents are known to have a stimulating effect, as the following lines from the Pashto poem "Lover's Jealousy," by the Afghan poet Mirza Rahchan Kayil (Hussein Izzat Rafi, fl. 19th cent.), show:

Oh, this scent floating from your neck, your breasts, your arms;
That circles about your thighs and your little belly;
This scent that is fed for ever and for ever
From two shady flasks under your bright arms,
I carry the scent of your body about with me.

(Edward Powys Mathers, *Coloured Stars: Versions of Fifty Asiatic Love Poems* [Oxford: Blackwell, 1919], 37).

Body odor was not something to be frowned upon; it was recognized as a powerful aphrodisiac. Napoléon (1769–1821) is said to have famously written to his wife, Joséphine, from Egypt, "Don't wash, I am coming!" (*Ne te lave pas, j'arrive!*).

DON'T GO

Morikā was a woman poet. Nothing else is known of her.

HIDDEN FINGERNAIL MARKS

Nothing is known of Murāri (9th cent.).

4–5: Women made themselves attractive by painting figures on their faces and breasts with sandalwood paste or other fragrant substances. Compare with Kālidāsa's *The Origin of the Young God* (*Kumārasaṃbhava*, 8.10).

HER FACE

Rājaśekhara (9th–10th cent.) was a prolific poet at the court of King Mahendrapāla of Kānyakubja. He is the author of *A Study of Poetry* (*Kāvyamīmāṃsā*).

WHAT THE YOUNG WIFE SAID TO THE TRAVELER

Rudraṭa (9th cent.) wrote one of the earliest works on poetics, *Ornament in Poetry* (*Kāvyālaṅkāra*). For a note on "traveler" poems, see the introduction, pp. xxxi–xxxiii.

GIRL DRAWING WATER FROM A WELL

Śaraṇa (12th cent.) was a poet at the court of King Lakṣmaṇasenā (r. 1179–1205) of Bengal.

2: It was not unusual for an outcaste woman, like the girl here, to not cover her breasts with a bodice. One end of the cloth was wrapped over the shoulder and often tucked in at the waist.

THE EMPTY ROAD

Nothing is known of Siddhoka. This is his only poem that has survived. The poem employs the motif of a woman whose husband is gone abroad or on a journey (*proṣitabhartṛkā*), one of the eight heroines of erotic poetry. The critic Viśvanātha (14th cent.) defines her thus (VSD 3.84):

> The woman, who suffers the pangs of love
> because her lord is away in a distant land
> to further his many business interests,
> is known as the "one whose husband is abroad."

THEN AND NOW

Śīlābhaṭṭārikā was a woman poet who was, like Vidyā, probably from southern India.

3: The Vindhya mountains are a range in central India dividing the north from the south. For a reading of the poem, see the introduction, pp. xxxiv–xxxvi.

DRIVEN BY PASSION

Nothing is known of Sonnoka.

THE SMART GIRL

Śrīharṣa (12th cent.), not to be confused with King Harṣa (r. 606–647), the author of the play *Ratnāvalī* (A row of jewels), lived in Kānyakubja. One long poem, *The Story of Nala, King of Niṣadha* (*Naiṣadhacarita*), is attributed to him. "The Smart Girl" is similar to "She Doesn't Let Go of Her Pride" (p. 33).

SEA OF SHAME

Vallaṇa (fl. 900–1100) was a poet from Bengal; nothing else is known of him. His poem is echoed by the Maithil poet Vidyāpati (14th–15th cent.) in the following lines of his poem "With the last of my garments":

With the last of my garments
shame dropped from me, fluttered
to earth and lay discarded at my feet.
My lover's body became
the only covering I needed.

(Edward C. Dimock Jr. and Denise Levertov, trans., *In Praise of Krishna: Songs from the Bengali* [Garden City, N.Y.: Doubleday, 1967], 27).

6: "God of love" is the translation of *manasijo devaḥ* (literally, "the mind-born god"), one of the epithets of Kāma. Śiva burned Kāma to ashes when the latter disturbed his meditation. He later brought him back to life when he discovered that the world was dying. In iconography, Kāma is represented as a young man with a bow and arrows tipped with flowers and riding on a parrot.

ON THE GRASS

Two travelers, a man and a woman, run into each other on the way. The woman is resting by a pond. Seeing her alone, the man comes on to her.

THE ESSENCE OF POETRY

An anonymous Telugu poem, "Not Entirely Hidden," echoes Vallaṇa's poem. Both poems offer a definition of poetry in terms of what is half unseen and therefore all the more seductive—a woman's "half-uncovered breasts."

Not entirely hidden,
like the enormous breasts of those Gujarati women,
and not open to view,
like a Tamil woman's breasts,
but rather,
like the supple, half-uncovered breasts
of a Telugu girl,
neither concealed nor exposed:

that's how a poem should be composed.
Anything else
is a joke.

(Velcheru Narayana Rao and David Shulman, trans., *A Poem at the Right Moment: Remembered Verses from Premodern South India* [Berkeley: University of California Press, 1998], 33).

PORING OVER A BOOK

Nothing is known of Varāha. Compare with the Chinese poet Bai Juyi's (772–846) poem "Old Age," especially the following lines:

The dull eye is closed ere night comes;
The idle head, still uncombed at noon.
Propped on a staff, sometimes a walk abroad;
Or all day sitting with closed doors.
One dares not look in the mirror's polished face;
One cannot read small-letter books.

(Arthur Waley, *Translations from the Chinese* [New York: Knopf, 1941], 253).

HOLLOW PLEASURES

Vidyā, Vijjā, or Vijjakā (fl. 7th–9th cent.) was a woman poet. Nothing else is known of her. It is possible that she was from southern India, as the following poem (JS 4.96) from Bhagadatta Jalhaṇa's *A String of Pearls of Fine Verses* (*Sūktimuktāvalī*, 13th cent.) by her suggests:

> Not knowing me, Vijjakā,
> dark as the petal of the blue lotus,
> it is quite foolish of Daṇḍin to say
> the Goddess of Poetry is white.

Vidyā claimed to be the goddess of poetry, Sarasvatī incarnate, a claim endorsed by the poet Rājaśekhara, who praised her as the "Kannada goddess of speech" (JS 4.93). Daṇḍin (7th cent.) was a poet at the court of the Pallava king Narasiṃhavarman I (r. 630–668) of Kanchipuram in Tamil Nadu. He is best known for his prose narrative *Tales of the Ten Princes* (*Daśakumāracarita*), and for an influential work on poetics, *The Mirror of Poetry* (*Kāvyādarśa*). Vidyā was an exceptional woman who probably enjoyed royal patronage.

COMPLAINT

For a reading of the poem, see the introduction, pp. xxiv–xxvi.

THE RIVERBANK

The woman anticipates the marks of her lover's fingernails on her breasts as she sets out to meet him under the pretext of fetching water from the river for her husband. A wife is expected to be faithful to her husband. The poem subverts that expectation. The poet resorts to innuendo (*vyañjanā*) to refer to the wife's infidelity. She does not spell it out, since it would offend social conventions. The image of the "reeds/whose broken shoots may scrape against my breasts" is a metaphor for the lover's fingernail marks on her breasts. For fingernail marks, see note (pp. 101–102) on "That's How I Saw Her."

1: The woman refers to her husband as "the child's father," as it was customary for women to avoid calling their husbands by their names.

5: "Gamboge" is the translation of *tamāla* (*Xanthochymus pictorious* Roxb.), a black-barked tree that grows on riverbanks.

THE BED

Vikaṭanitambā (9th cent.) was a woman poet. Short of describing the lovemaking, the poet offers telling details surrounding the event: the knot holding the woman's skirt gives way, and the skirt itself collapses to the floor. The tactile images are themselves erotic: "bed," "knot," "skirt," "hips," "cords," "belt," and "arms." Orgasm renders the woman speechless, erasing the memory of their lovemaking.

For a note on the poet's name, see the introduction, p. xliii.

A WORD OF ADVICE

The exhortation to "Throw caution to the wind:/squeeze her hard when the two of you are alone" must be understood in the context of the prohibition against touching. Notwithstanding the risk of breaking a social taboo, the man is told to establish physical contact with the girl as the first step toward possessing her. Though the comparison of a girl to sugarcane might appear somewhat unflattering today, it is quite suggestive, especially if we keep in mind the belief that the god of love Kāma's bow is made of sugarcane.

FAR FROM HOME

Yogeśvara (800–900) was a poet from Bengal. For a note on Yogeśvara's realistic descriptions of country scenes, see the introduction, pp. xli–xlii.

5: The kadamba tree (*Anthocephalus cadamba*), with yellow ball-shaped fragrant blossoms, flowers in the monsoon (June to September). Kadamba woods are a favorite of the god Kṛṣṇa and the goddess Durgā.

I have chosen the poems translated in this volume from the following works; the editions of the texts are listed in the bibliography.

1. The *Amaruśataka* (Amaru's one hundred poems, 7th cent.) is the foremost anthology of Sanskrit erotic verse. It is said, "Just one verse of Amaru equals one hundred good works." The words "one hundred" in the title should not be taken literally; they only mean "many." In fact, the number of poems varies from 90 to 115 in the "450 odd manuscripts." Traditionally attributed to Amaru, the anthology is the work of several writers. It was first published, with the *Kāmadā* commentary of Ravicandra, in 1808 in Calcutta.
2. Bhartṛhari's *Śatakatrayādi-subhāṣitasaṃgraḥ* (Three hundred poems: A collection of well-turned verse, ca. 400) comprises epigrams on right conduct, love, and asceticism that are unmatched by any other poet, except Kālidāsa. Edited by William Carey, it was first published in 1803 in Srirampur, Bengal.
3. Bhāskara II's *Līlāvatī* (The beautiful, 12th cent.) is a classic work on arithmetic written in verse. Edited and translated into English by Henry Thomas Colebrooke, it was first published in 1817 in London.
4. Bhavabhūti's *Mālatīmādhava* (Mālatī and Mādhava, 8th cent.) is one of three plays of the poet that have survived. Edited by Ramakrishna Gopal Bhandarkar, it was first published in 1876 in Bombay.
5. Bilhaṇa's *Caurapañcāśikā* (Fifty poems of a thief of love, 11th cent.) is a poetic sequence. Edited by Peter von Bohlen, it was first published in 1833 in Berlin.
6. The *Subhāṣitahārāvalī* (A garland of well-turned verse, 17th cent., in MS) was compiled by Harikavi (Bhānubhaṭṭa), a poet at the court of the Marāṭhā king Saṃbhājī (r. 1680–1689).

7. Jagannātha Paṇḍitarāja's *Paṇḍitarājakāvyasaṃgrah* (The complete poetical works of Paṇḍitarāja, 17th cent.). Edited by Aryendra Sharma, it was first published in1958 in Hyderabad, Andhra Pradesh.
8. Kṣemendra's *Aucityavicāracarcā* (A critical discourse on propriety, 11th cent.) is a landmark text in Sanskrit poetics. Edited by Pandit Durgaprasad and Kasinath Pandurang Parab, it was first published in 1886 in Bombay.
9. Kālidāsa's *Abhijñānaśākuntala* (Śakuntalā and the ring of recollection, 4th–5th cent.) is one of three plays of the poet that have survived. Edited by Antoine-Léonard de Chézy, it was first published in 1820 in Paris.
10. Kālidāsa's *Mālavikāgnimitra* (Mālavikā and Agnimitra, 4th–5th cent.) is one of three plays of the poet that have survived. Edited by Otto Fredrik Tullberg, it was first published in 1840 in Bonn. Tullberg's edition was unsatisfactory. It was superseded by Shankar P. Pandit's edition, with the commentary of Kāṭayavema, published in 1869 in Bombay.
11. The Rig Veda (The knowledge of the praise songs, 1200–900 B.C.E.), comprising 1,028 hymns, is the oldest literature of the Indo-European peoples. Edited by Friedrich Max Müller in six volumes, it was first published in 1849–1874 in London.
12. The *Ṛtusaṃhāra* (The cycle of the seasons, 2nd–5th cent.) is incorrectly attributed to Kālidāsa; it is the work of an unknown poet. It comprises 153 poems in praise of the seasons. It is the earliest surviving example of the genre known as poetry describing the seasons (*ṛtuvarṇanakāvya*). Edited by "some unknown scholar/scholars" under the supervision of Sir William Jones, it was first published in 1792 in Bengali script in Calcutta.
13. The *Śārṅgadharapaddhati* (Śārṅgadhara's guide to poetry, 14th cent.) comprises 4,689 poems. About 271 poets are named; the rest are anonymous. Edited by Peter Peterson, it was first published in 1888 in Bombay.
14. The *Śṛṅgāratilaka* (The mark of love) is incorrectly attributed to Kālidāsa; it is the work of an unknown poet. It comprises thirty-one

poems on love. Edited by Johann Gildemeister, it was first published in 1841 in Bonn.

15. The *Subhāṣitāvalī* (A sequence of well-turned verses, 16th cent.), compiled by Vallabhadeva, comprises 3,527 poems. About 350 poets are named; the rest are anonymous. Edited by Peter Peterson and Pandit Durgaprasad, it was first published in 1886 in Bombay.
16. The *Subhāṣitaratnakoṣa* (A treasury of well-turned verse, 11th cent.), compiled by the Buddhist abbot Vidyākara of the Jagaddāla Monastery, founded by the Pāla king Rāmapāla (r. 1077–1120) in Varendra in what is now Bangladesh, comprises 1,738 poems. About 220 poets are named; the rest are anonymous. Edited by D. D. Kosambi and V. V. Gokhale, it was first published in 1957 in Cambridge, Massachusetts.

SOURCES OF POEMS

ABBREVIATIONS

For details concerning the following works, see the notes to the poems and the bibliography.

AS	*Amaruśataka* (Nirnaya Sagara ed.)
ASVR	*Amaruśataka* (Vemabhūpāla's recension)
BC	Bilhaṇa, *Caurapañcāśikā* (northern recension)
BL	Bhāskara, *Līlāvatī* (Colebrooke's trans.)
BM	Bhavabhūti, *Mālatīmādhava*
BS	Bhartṛhari, *Śatakatrayādi-subhāṣitasaṃgraḥ*
HS	Harikavi, *Subhāṣitahārāvalī*
JPK	Jagannātha Paṇḍitarāja, *Paṇḍitarājakāvyasaṃgraḥ*
JS	Bhagadatta Jalhaṇa, *Sūktimuktāvalī*
KA	Kṣemendra, *Aucityavicāracarcā*
KM	Kālidāsa, *Mālavikāgnimitra*
KS	Kālidāsa, *Abhijñānaśākuntala*
RP	Rājaśekhara Sūri, *Prabandhakoṣa*
RS	*Ṛtusaṃhāra*
RV	Rig Veda
SP	Śārṅgadhara, *Śārṅgadharapaddhati*
ST	*Śṛṅgāratilaka*
UK	Udbhaṭa, *Kāvyālaṃkārasārasaṃgraḥ*

VS Vallabhadeva, *Subhāṣitāvalī*
VSD Viśvanātha, *Sāhityadarpaṇa*
VSR Vidyākara, *Subhāṣitaratnakoṣa*

The abbreviations following the titles refer to the Sanskrit texts, and the numbers refer to the poems within each text.

ABHINANDA

That's How I Saw Her [VSR 589]

AMARU

Who Needs the Gods? [AS 3]
In a Hundred Places [AS 11],
A Taste of Ambrosia [AS 36]
Pincers [AS 74]
The Bride [AS 90]

ANON

Lovers' Quarrel [AS 23]
The Pledge [AS 43]
A Lover's Welcome [AS 45]
Regret [AS 58]
Stonehearted [AS 59]
Feigning Sleep [AS 82]
Remorse [AS 92]
Walking the Street by Her House [AS 100]
The Sheets [AS 107]
A Woman Wronged [AS 114]
Aubade [RS 5.11]
Like the Wheels of a Chariot [RV 10.10.7]
The Word [RV 10.71.4]
An Invitation [SP 3918]
The Traveler [ST 12]
The Devoted Wife [VS 1049]
The Kingdom's Happiness [VS 1476]

Hair [VS 1481]
Wild Nights [VS 2151]
Thank Offering [VS 2366]
At the Cremation Ground [VS 3195]
On a Rainy Day [VSR 261]
When Winter Comes [VSR 312]
Jewels [VSR 559]
The Creaking Bed [VSR 573]
She Protests Too Much [VSR 587]
She Doesn't Let Go of Her Pride [VSR 690]
The Ways of Love [VSR 696]
A Lover's Word [VSR 830]
The Hawk [VSR 1150]
A Needle [VSR 1307]
Time Wasted [VSR 1469]
The Scholar's Life [VSR 1478]
Foolish Heart [VSR 1503]
Supreme Bliss [VSR 1624]

BĀṆA

In a Corner of the Village Shrine [VSR 1305]

BHARTṚHARI

Wise Men [BS 88]
Poets' Excesses [BS 108]
The Love Game [BS 124]
Hips [BS 147]
Fear of Death [BS 153]
Desire Alone [BS 156]
Adoration of Woman [BS 159]
The Poet Speaks to the King [BS 166]
Contentment [BS 190]
Man's Life [BS 200]
Old Age [BS 242]
White Flag [BS 323]

BHĀSKARA II

Elementary Arithmetic [BL 54]

BHAVABHŪTI

The Critic Scorned [BM 1.6]

BHĀVAKADEVĪ

Bitter Harvest [AS 69]

BHOJA

Scrambling Out of the Water [VSR 1160]

BILHAṆA

Bite Marks [BC 13]
In Life After Life [BC 22]
All for Love [BC 23]

DEVAGUPTA

Drumbeats [AS 31]

DHARMAKĪRTI

The Way [VSR 1729]

JAGANNĀTHA PAṆḌITARĀJA

Indra's Heaven [JPK 585]

JAGHANACAPALĀ

Wife [VSR 825]

KĀLIDĀSA

Flight of the Deer [KS 1.7]
Such Innocent Moves [KM 4.15]
Blessed Sleep [VSR 806]

KARṆOTPALA

The Lamp [VSR 570]

KEŚAṬA

The Camel [VSR 512]

KṢEMENDRA

All Eyes on the Door [KA 35]

KṢITĪŚA

The Red Seal [VSR 758]

KUMĀRADĀSA

Alba [KA 24]

KUṬALĀ

Furtive Lovemaking [HS 79]

MĀGHA

The Art of Poetry [KA 30]

Scent [VSR 627]

MAHODADHI

Stop Being Willful [VSR 654]

MORIKĀ

Don't Go [VS 1053]

MURĀRI

Hidden Fingernail Marks [VSR 634]

An Actor in a Farce [VSR 1526]

RĀJAPUTRA PARPAṬI

Blow Out the Lamp [VS 2053]

RĀJAŚEKHARA

Her Face [VSR 797]

RUDRAṬA

What the Young Wife Said to the Traveler [VSR 812]

ŚARAṆA

Girl Drawing Water from a Well [VSR 1152]

SIDDHOKA

The Empty Road [AS 76]

ŚĪLĀBHAṬṬĀRIKĀ

Then and Now [VSR 815]

SONNOKA

Driven by Passion [VSR 581]

ŚRĪHARṢA

The Smart Girl [AS 18]

In Her Direction [AS 99]

VALLAṆA

Sea of Shame [VSR 568]

On the Grass [VSR 822]

The Essence of Poetry [VSR 1705]

VARĀHA

Poring Over a Book [VSR 1179]

VIDYĀ

Hollow Pleasures [VS 1175]

Complaint [VSR 574]

The Riverbank [VSR 807]

VIKAṬANITAMBĀ

The Bed [AS 101]

A Word of Advice [VS 1401]

YOGEŚVARA

Far from Home [VSR 220]

When the Rains Come [VSR 221]

BIBLIOGRAPHY

PRIMARY WORKS

Abhijñānaśākuntala of Kālidāsa, with the commentary of Rāghava Bhaṭṭa. Ed. Narayan Ram Acharya. 12th ed. Bombay: Nirnaya Sagara Press, 1958.

Amaruśataka, with the Sanskrit commentary the *Rasikasañjīvinī* of Arjunavarmadeva. Ed. Pandit Durgaprasad and Kasinath Pandurang Parab. Bombay: Nirnaya Sagara Press, 1889.

Amaruśataka, with the Sanskrit commentary the *Śṛṅgāradīpikā* of Vemabhūpāla. Ed. and trans. Chintaman Ramchandra Devadhar. 1959. Reprint, New Delhi: Motilal Banarsidass, 1984.

Anaṅgaraṅga of Kalyāṇamalla. Edited, with a Hindi translation and commentary, by Ram Sagar Tripathi. Delhi: Chaukhamba Sanskrit Pratishthan, 1988.

Aucityavicāracarcā of Kṣemendra. Ed. Pandit Dhundhiraja Sastri. Haridas Sanskrit Series, no. 25. Varanasi: Chaukhamba Sanskrit Series Office, 1933.

Kāmasūtra of Vātsyāyana, with the Sanskrit commentary *Jayamaṅgalā* of Śrī Yaśodhara Indrapada. Edited, with the Hindi commentary *Jaya*, by Devadatta Sastri. Kashi Sanskrit Series, no. 29. Varanasi: Chaukhamba Sanskrit Series Office, 1964.

Kavikaṇṭābharaṇa of Kṣemendra. Ed. Pandit Dhundhiraja Sastri. Vols. 10 and 11. Banaras: Chaukhamba Sanskrit Series Office, 1933.

Kāvyālaṃkārasārasaṃgraḥ of Udbhaṭa. Edited, with the commentary the *Laghuvṛtti* of Indurāja, by Narayana Daso Banhatti. Bombay Sanskrit and Prākrit Series, no. 79. 2nd ed. Poona: Bhandarkar Oriental Research Institute, 1982.

Kāvyamīmāṃsa of Rājaśekhara. Ed. K. S. Ramaswamy Sastri Siromani. Gaekwad's Oriental Series, no. 1. 3rd ed. 1916. Reprint, Baroda: Oriental Institute, Maharaja Sayajirao University of Baroda, 1934.

Līlāvatī of Bhāskara II (Algebra, with Arithmetic and Mensuration, from the Sanskrit of *Brahmagupta and Bhāskara*). Ed. and trans. Henry Thomas Colebrooke. London: Murray, 1817.

Love Song of the Dark Lord: Jayadeva's "Gītagovinda." Ed. and trans. Barbara Stoler Miller. New York: Columbia University Press, 1977.

Mālatīmādhava of Bhavabhūti. Ed. Michael Coulson. Revised by Roderick Sinclair. New Delhi: Oxford University Press, 1989.

Mālavikāgnimitra of Kālidāsa, with Kāṭayavema's commentary. Ed. Narayan Ram Acharya. 9th ed. Bombay: Nirnaya Sagara Press, 1950.

Mṛcchakaṭika of Śūdraka. Edited, with the commentary of Pṛthvīdhara, by Kasinath Pandurang Parab. Revised by Vasudev Laksman Sastri Pansikar. 6th ed. Bombay: Nirnaya Sagara Press, 1926.

Paṇḍitarājakāvyasaṃgraḥ. Ed. Aryendra Sharma. Hyderabad: Sanskrit Academy, 1958.

Phantasies of a Love-Thief: The Caurapañcāśikā Attributed to Bilhaṇa. Ed. and trans. Barbara Stoler Miller. New York: Columbia University Press, 1971.

Prabandhakoṣa of Rājaśekhara Sūri. Edited, with a Hindi translation, by Jina Vijaya. Singhi Jain Series, no. 6. Santiniketan, West Bengal: Adhisthata-Singhi Jaina Jnanapitha, 1935.

Rig Veda: A Metrically Restored Text with an Introduction and Notes. Ed. Barend A. van Nooten and Gary B. Holland. Harvard Oriental Series 50. Cambridge, Mass.: Department of Sanskrit and Indian Studies, Harvard University, 1994.

Ṛtusaṃhāra, including the commentary of Maṇirāma, and *Śṛṅgāratilaka*. Ed. Vasudev Laksman Sastri Pansikar. 4th ed. Bombay: Nirnaya Sagara Press, 1913.

Sāhityadarpaṇa of Śrī Viśvanātha Kavirāja. Edited, with a commentary, by Pandit Sri Krishna Mohan Thakur. Kashi Sanskrit Series 145. 3rd ed. Varanasi: Chaukhamba Sanskrit Series Office, 1967.

Śārṅgadharapaddhati, Volume 1: The Text. Ed. Peter Peterson. Bombay Sanskrit Series, no. 37. Bombay: Government Central Book Depot, 1888.

Śatakatrayādi-subhāṣitasaṃgraḥ of Bhartṛhari. Ed. D. D. Kosambi. Singhi Jain Series, no. 23. Bombay: Bharatiya Vidya Bhavan, 1948.

Subhāṣitahārāvalī [MS]. Compiled by Harikavi. Cited in *The Contribution of Women to Sanskrit Literature, Volume 2: Sanskrit Poetesses*, part A. Ed. Jatindra Bimal Chaudhuri. Calcutta, 1941.

Subhāṣitaratnakoṣa. Compiled by Vidyākara. Ed. D. D. Kosambi and V. V. Gokhale. Harvard Oriental Series 42. Cambridge, Mass.: Harvard University Press, 1957.

Subhāṣitāvalī. Compiled by Vallabhadeva. Ed. Peter Peterson and Pandit Durgaprasad. Revised by Raghunath Damodar Karmarkar. Bombay Sanskrit and Prākrit Series, no. 31. 2nd ed. Poona: Bhandarkar Oriental Research Institute, 1961.

Sūktimuktāvalī. Compiled by Bhagadatta Jalhaṇa. Ed. Embar Krishnamacharya. Gaekwad's Oriental Series, no. 82. Baroda: Oriental Institute, Maharaja Sayajirao University of Baroda, 1938.

WORKS IN TRANSLATION

Brough, John, trans. *Poems from the Sanskrit*. Harmondsworth, U.K.: Penguin, 1968.

Heifetz, Hank, trans. *The Origin of the Young God: Kālidāsa's "Kumārasaṃbhava."* Berkeley: University of California Press, 1985.

Ingalls, Daniel H. H., trans. *An Anthology of Sanskrit Court Poetry: Vidyākara's "Subhāṣitaratnakoṣa."* Harvard Oriental Series 44. Cambridge, Mass.: Harvard University Press, 1965.

Love Lyrics by Amaru, Bhartṛhari, and Bilhaṇa. Translated by Greg Bailey and Richard Gombrich. Clay Sanskrit Library. New York: New York University Press; John and Jennifer Clay Foundation, 2005.

Merwin, W. S., and J. Moussaieff Masson, trans. *Sanskrit Love Poetry*. New York: Columbia University Press, 1977.

Miller, Barbara Stoler, trans. *The Hermit and the Love-Thief: Sanskrit Poems of Bhartrihari and Bilhaṇa*. New York: Columbia University Press, 1978.

Nathan, Leonard, trans. *The Transport of Love: The Meghadūta of Kālidāsa*. Berkeley: University of California Press, 1976.

Rao, Velcheru Narayana, and David Shulman, trans. *A Poem at the Right Moment: Remembered Verses from Premodern South India*. Berkeley: University of California Press, 1998.

Rückert, Friedrich, trans. *Die hundert Strophen des Amaru*. Hanover: Orient-Buchhandlung Heinz Lafaire, 1925.

Selby, Martha Ann, trans. and ed. *Grow Long, Blessed Night: Love Poems from Classical India*. New York: Oxford University Press, 2000.

SECONDARY WORKS

Ānandavardhana. *The "Dhvanyāloka" with the "Locana" of Abhinavagupta*. Translated by Daniel H. H. Ingalls, Jeffrey Moussaieff Masson, and M. V. Patwardhan. Harvard Oriental Series 49. Cambridge, Mass.: Harvard University Press, 1990.

Bharata. *The Nāṭyaśāstra*. Translated by Adya Rangacharya. Rev. ed. New Delhi: Munshiram Manoharlal, 1996.

Bloch, Iwan. *Odoratus Sexualis: A Scientific and Literary Study of Sexual Scents and Erotic Perfumes*. New York: Panurge Press, 1934.

Borooah, Anundoram. *Prosody*. Gauhati: Publication Board, Assam, 1975.

Bronner, Yigal, David Shulman, and Gary Tubb, eds. *Innovations and Turning Points: Toward a History of Kāvya Literature*. South Asia Research. New Delhi: Oxford University Press, 2014.

Brown, Clarence, and W. S. Merwin, trans. *The Selected Poems of Osip Mandelstam*. New York: New York Review Books, 2004.

Catullus. *The Poems of Catullus*. Translated by Horace Gregory. New York: Grove Press, 1956.

Cheung, Martha P. Y., ed. *An Anthology of Chinese Discourse on Translation, Volume 1: From Earliest Times to the Buddhist Project*. Manchester, U.K.: St Jerome, 2006.

Clifton, Lucille. *The Collected Poems of Lucille Clifton, 1965–2010*. Ed. Kevin Young and Michael S. Glaser. Rochester, N.Y.: BOA Editions, 2012.

Coomaraswamy, Ananda K. "Status of Indian Women." In *The Dance of Shiva: Fourteen Indian Essays*, 98–123. Rev. ed. New York: Noonday Press, 1956.

Daniélou, Alain, trans. *The Complete Kāma Sūtra: The First Unabridged Modern Translation of the Classic Indian Text*. Rochester, Vt.: Park Street Press, 1994.

Das Saptaçatakam des Hâla. Ed. Albrecht Weber. Abhandlungen für die Kunde des Morgenlandes, Band 7, No. 4. Leipzig: Brockhaus, 1881.

De, S. K. *Sanskrit Poetics as a Study of Aesthetic*. Berkeley: University of California Press, 1963.

Di Giacomo, Salvatore. *Love Poems: A Selection*. Translated by Frank J. Palescandolo. Essential Poets 79. Toronto: Guernica, 1999.

Dimmitt, Cornelia, and J. A. B. van Buitenen, eds. and trans. *Classical Hindu Mythology*. Philadelphia: Temple University Press, 1978.

Dimock, Edward C., et al. *The Literatures of India: An Introduction*. Chicago: University of Chicago Press, 1974.

Dimock, Edward C., Jr., and Denise Levertov, trans. *In Praise of Krishna: Songs from the Bengali*. Garden City, N.Y.: Doubleday, 1967.

Donne, John. *John Donne's Poetry*. Ed. Arthur L. Clements. 2nd ed. New York: Norton, 1992.

Duncan-Jones, Katherine, ed. *Shakespeare's Sonnets*. The Arden Shakespeare. London: Nelson, 1997.

Edgerton, Franklin. "Indirect Suggestion in Poetry: A Hindu Theory of Literary Aesthetics." *Proceedings of the American Philosophical Society* 76, no. 5 (1936): 687–706.

Ellis, Havelock. *Studies in the Psychology of Sex, Volume 4: Sexual Selection in Man*. Philadelphia: Davis, 1914.

Emeneau, M. B. "Signed Verses by Sanskrit Poets." *Indian Linguistics* 16 (November 1955): 41–52.

Fitts, Dudley, trans. *Poems from the Greek Anthology*. New York: New Directions, 1938.

Gerow, Edwin. *A Glossary of Indian Figures of Speech*. The Hague: Mouton, 1971.

Hallisey, Charles, trans. *Therīgāthā: Poems of the First Buddhist Women*. Murty Classical Library of India 3. Cambridge, Mass.: Harvard University Press, 2015.

Ingalls. Daniel H. H. "General Introduction." In *An Anthology of Sanskrit Court Poetry: Vidyākara's "Subhāṣitaratnakoṣa,"* 1–53. Harvard Oriental Series 44. Cambridge, Mass.: Harvard University Press, 1965.

——. "A Sanskrit Poetry of Village and Field: Yogeśvara and His Fellow Poets." *Journal of the American Oriental Society* 74, no. 3 (July–September 1954): 119–31.

Keegan, Paul, ed. *The New Penguin Book of English Verse*. London: Penguin, 2001.

Kuṟuntokai (An anthology of short poems). Compiled by Pūrikkō. Ed. U. Ve. Caminataiyar. Annamalai Nagar: Annamalai University, 1983.

Lao Tzu: Tao Te Ching. Translated by D. C. Lau. Harmondsworth, U.K.: Penguin, 1963.

Lienhard, Siegfried. *A History of Classical Poetry: Sanskrit, Pāli, Prākrit*. A History of Indian Literature, vol. 3, fasc. 1. Ed. Jan Gonda. Wiesbaden: Harrassowitz, 1984.

Mathers, Edward Powys. *Coloured Stars: Versions of Fifty Asiatic Love Poems*. Oxford: Blackwell, 1919.

Meyer, Johann Jakob. *Sexual Life in Ancient India: A Study in the Comparative History of Indian Culture*. 2 vols. London: Routledge and Kegan Paul, 1930.

Mitra, Arati. *The Origin and Development of Sanskrit Metrics*. Calcutta: Asiatic Society, 1989.

Ovid. *The Metamorphoses*. Translated by Horace Gregory. New York: Viking, 1958.

Ploss, Hermann Heinrich, Max Bartels, and Paul Bartels. *Woman: An Historical, Gynaecological, and Anthropological Compendium*. Ed. Eric John Dingwall. 3 vols. London: Heinemann, 1935.

Pollock, Sheldon I. *Aspects of Versification in Sanskrit Lyric Poetry*. American Oriental Series, vol. 61. New Haven, Conn.: American Oriental Society, 1977.

—. *The Language of the Gods in the World of Men: Sanskrit, Culture, and Power in Premodern India*. Berkeley: University of California Press, 2006.

—, trans. and ed. *A Rasa Reader: Classical Indian Aesthetics*. New York: Columbia University Press, 2016.

—. "Sanskrit Literary Culture from the Inside Out." In *Literary Cultures in History: Reconstructions from South Asia*, Ed. Sheldon Pollock, 39–130. Berkeley: University of California Press, 2003.

Puṟanāṉūṟu (The four hundred heroic songs). Compiled by Peruntēvaṉār. Ed. Auvai Cu. Turaicamippillai. 2 vols. Tirunelveli: South India Saiva-siddhanta Publishing Works Society, 1967–1972.

Raghavan, V. *The Number of Rasas*. 3rd rev. ed. Madras: Adyar Library and Research Centre, 1975.

Rao, Velcheru Narayana, ed. and trans. *Hibiscus on the Lake: Twentieth-Century Telugu Poetry from India*. Madison: University of Wisconsin Press, 2003.

Rexroth, Kenneth, trans. *Poems from the Greek Anthology*. Ann Arbor: University of Michigan Press, 1962.

Richlin, Amy. *The Garden of Priapus: Sexuality and Aggression in Roman Humor*. New Haven, Conn.: Yale University Press, 1983.

Russell, Ralph, ed. *The Oxford India Ghalib: Life, Letters and Ghazals*. New Delhi: Oxford University Press, 2003.

A Sanskrit-English Dictionary. Compiled by Sir Monier Monier-Williams. Oxford: Clarendon Press, 1899.

Sanskrit-Wörterbuch. Compiled by Otto Böhtlingk and Rudolf Roth. 7 vols. St. Petersburg: Kaiserliche Akademie der Wissenschaften, 1855–1875.

Santos, Sherod. *Greek Lyric Poetry: A New Translation*. New York: Norton, 2005.

Schumann, H. W. *The Historical Buddha*. Translated by M. O'C. Walshe. London: Arkana, 1989.

Schwab, Raymond. *The Oriental Renaissance: Europe's Rediscovery of India and the East, 1680–1880*. Translated by Gene Patterson-Black and Victor Reinking. New York: Columbia University Press, 1984.

Sullerot, Evelyne. *Women on Love: Eight Centuries of Feminine Writing*. Translated by Helen R. Lane. Garden City, N.Y.: Doubleday, 1979.

Thampi, G. B. Mohan. "Rasa as Aesthetic Experience." *Journal of Aesthetics and Art Criticism* 24, no. 1 (1965): 75–79.

Thera- and Therī-Gāthā: Stanzas Ascribed to Elders of the Buddhist Order of Recluses. Ed. Hermann Oldenburg and Richard Pischel. Pāli Text Society. 2nd ed. London: Luzac, 1966.

Waley, Arthur. *Translations from the Chinese*. New York: Knopf, 1941.

Warder, A. K. *Indian Kavya Literature*. 7 vols. Delhi: Motilal Banarsidass, 1972–2004.

Winternitz, Maurice. *A History of Indian Literature*. 3 vols. Vol. 1 translated by S. Ketkar. Vol. 2 translated by S. Ketkar and H. Kohn. Vol. 3, fasc. 1, translated by H. Kohn. Calcutta: University of Calcutta, 1927–1949. Vol. 3, parts 1 and 2, translated by Subhadra Jha. Delhi: Motilal Banarsidass, 1963–1967.

Woolf, Virginia. *A Room of One's Own*. San Diego: Harcourt, Brace, Jovanovich, 1957.

Wordsworth, William. *Selected Poems*. Ed. John O. Hayden. London: Penguin, 1994.

Yeats, W. B. *The Collected Works of W. B. Yeats, Volume 1: The Poems*. Ed. Richard J. Finneran. Rev. ed. New York: Macmillan, 1989.

Yevtushenko, Yevgeny, comp. *Twentieth-Century Russian Poetry: Silver and Steel; An Anthology*. Ed. Albert C. Todd and Max Hayward. New York: Doubleday, 1993.

CREDITS

"'The Waistband of Hermione' by Asklepiades of Samos," from *Greek Lyric Poetry: A New Translation,* translated by Sherod Santos. Copyright © 2005 by Sherod Santos. Reprinted by permission of W. W. Norton & Company, Inc.

"'The Jewel Stairs' Grievance' by Li Po" by Ezra Pound, from *Translations.* Copyright © 1963 by Ezra Pound. Reprinted by permission of New Directions Publishing Corp.

"'Doris' by Dioscorides of Alexandria," translated by Amy Richlin, from *The Garden of Priapus: Sexuality and Aggression in Roman Humor* (New Haven, Conn.: Yale University Press, 1983). Copyright © 1983 by Amy Richlin. Reprinted by permission of the author.

"'The Unfaithful Wife' by Philodemus of Gadara," from *Poems from the Greek Anthology*, translated by Kenneth Rexroth. Copyright © 1962 by Kenneth Rexroth. Reprinted by permission of the University of Michigan Press.

"'To His Mistress' by Asklepiades of Samos," by Dudley Fitts, translated by Dudley Fitts, from *Poems from the Greek Anthology*. Copyright © 1956 by New Directions Publishing Corp. Reprinted by permission of New Directions Publishing Corp.

"'Tryst' by Duvvuri Ramireddy," from *Hibiscus on the Lake: Twentieth-Century Telugu Poetry from India,* translated by Velcheru Narayana

Rao. Copyright © 2003 by the Regents of the University of Wisconsin System. Reprinted by permission of the University of Wisconsin Press.

"Not Entirely Hidden," from *A Poem at the Right Moment: Remembered Verses from Premodern South India*, translated by Velcheru Narayana Rao and David Shulman. Copyright © 1998 by the Regents of the University of California. Reprinted by permission of the University of California Press.

INDEX OF TITLES AND FIRST LINES

Titles are listed in *italic* type and first lines in roman.

INDEX

Authors are listed in ALL CAPS.

Merwin, W. S., xvi
Metamorphoses (Ovid), 110
mokṣa, xxvi
MORIKĀ, 78, 117
motif: creaking bed, 31, 106; flickering lamp, 69, 77, 114; stolen love, 115; untying the knot of a woman's skirt, xxv–xxvi, 71, 95; walking the street, 14, 103; woman offended, xxxiii; woman whose husband is abroad, 118
Mount Lu, xl
Mṛcchakaṭika of Śūdraka, xxx
muktaka, xx, xxiii
MURĀRI, 79, 80, 117
"My heartless lover, I hear" (Niṣpaṭa), xxxi
myth: churning the ocean, 102

Naiṣadhacarita of Śrīharṣa, 119
"Nannina" (Di Giacomo), 103
Napoléon, 117
Narasiṃhavarman I, King, 121
Niṣpaṭa, xxxi
"Not Entirely Hidden" (Anon), 120
"Not knowing me, Vijjakā" (Vidyā), 121

"Old Age" (Bai Juyi), 120
Ovid, 110

Paithan, xxxi
Pāli, xxxi, xxxix
Pāmara (ancient tribe of the Vindhya), xlii
Paṇḍitrāj Jagannāth (Marathi play by Vidyadhar Gokhale), 113
PARPAṬI, RĀJAPUTRA, 81
Pārvatī, 105
pathetic fallacy, xli
pathikaḥ, xxxi
patronage, xviii–xix, xliii–xlv, 107, 112, 114–115
Philodemus of Gadara, xxx
"Poem 6" (Catullus), 106
poetry: American, 109; Bengali, xxxiv; Chinese, xxvii–xxviii, xl–xli; definition of, xvii–xviii, 92, 120; devotional (*bhakti*), xxxiv; English, xxxv, xxxviii, xli–xlii, 107–109; French, 102; Greek, xxv–xxvi, xxix–xxx, xxxvii; Hebrew, xxii; Hindi, 113; Italian, 103; Latin, 106–110; Maithil, 119; Pāli, xxxix; Pashto, 116; Persian, 111; Prākrit, xxxi–xxxii; Russian, xliv, 116; Tamil, xliv, 116; Telugu, 112–113, 120; Urdu, 113
Pound, Ezra, xxvii
Prākrit, xix, xxxi–xxxii
Pratiṣṭhāna, xxxi
proṣitabhartṛkā, 118
Proverbs, xxii
pseudonyms, xliii
pubic hair, 105–106
Pulīndra (ancient tribe of the Vindhya), xlii

Rādhā (consort of Kṛṣṇa), xxix, xxxiv
Raghuvaṃśa of Kālidāsa, 114
rain, 28, 99–100, 123
RĀJAŚEKHARA, xviii, 82, 117
Ramakrishna Deva, 110
Ramireddy, Duvvuri, 112
Rao, Y. V., 113

TRANSLATIONS FROM THE ASIAN CLASSICS

Major Plays of Chikamatsu, tr. Donald Keene 1961

Four Major Plays of Chikamatsu, tr. Donald Keene. Paperback ed. only. 1961; rev. ed. 1997

Records of the Grand Historian of China, translated from the Shih chi of Ssu-ma Ch'ien, tr. Burton Watson, 2 vols. 1961

Instructions for Practical Living and Other Neo-Confucian Writings by Wang Yang-ming, tr. Wing-tsit Chan 1963

Hsün Tzu: Basic Writings, tr. Burton Watson, paperback ed. only. 1963; rev. ed. 1996

Chuang Tzu: Basic Writings, tr. Burton Watson, paperback ed. only. 1964; rev. ed. 1996

The Mahābhārata, tr. Chakravarthi V. Narasimhan. Also in paperback ed. 1965; rev. ed. 1997

The Manyōshū, Nippon Gakujutsu Shinkōkai edition 1965

Su Tung-p'o: Selections from a Sung Dynasty Poet, tr. Burton Watson. Also in paperback ed. 1965

Bhartrihari: Poems, tr. Barbara Stoler Miller. Also in paperback ed. 1967

Basic Writings of Mo Tzu, Hsün Tzu, and Han Fei Tzu, tr. Burton Watson. Also in separate paperback eds. 1967

The Awakening of Faith, Attributed to Aśvaghosha, tr. Yoshito S. Hakeda. Also in paperback ed. 1967

Reflections on Things at Hand: The Neo-Confucian Anthology, comp. Chu Hsi and Lü Tsu-ch'ien, tr. Wing-tsit Chan 1967

The Platform Sutra of the Sixth Patriarch, tr. Philip B. Yampolsky. Also in paperback ed. 1967

Essays in Idleness: The Tsurezuregusa of Kenkō, tr. Donald Keene. Also in paperback ed. 1967

The Pillow Book of Sei Shōnagon, tr. Ivan Morris, 2 vols. 1967

Two Plays of Ancient India: The Little Clay Cart and the Minister's Seal, tr. J. A. B. van Buitenen 1968

The Complete Works of Chuang Tzu, tr. Burton Watson 1968

The Romance of the Western Chamber (Hsi Hsiang chi), tr. S. I. Hsiung. Also in paperback ed. 1968

The Manyōshū, Nippon Gakujutsu Shinkōkai edition. Paperback ed. only. 1969

Records of the Historian: Chapters from the Shih chi of Ssu-ma Ch'ien, tr. Burton Watson. Paperback ed. only. 1969

Cold Mountain: 100 Poems by the T'ang Poet Han-shan, tr. Burton Watson. Also in paperback ed. 1970

Twenty Plays of the Nō Theatre, ed. Donald Keene. Also in paperback ed. 1970

Chūshingura: The Treasury of Loyal Retainers, tr. Donald Keene. Also in paperback ed. 1971; rev. ed. 1997

The Zen Master Hakuin: Selected Writings, tr. Philip B. Yampolsky 1971

Chinese Rhyme-Prose: Poems in the Fu Form from the Han and Six Dynasties Periods, tr. Burton Watson. Also in paperback ed. 1971

Kūkai: Major Works, tr. Yoshito S. Hakeda. Also in paperback ed. 1972

The Old Man Who Does as He Pleases: Selections from the Poetry and Prose of Lu Yu, tr. Burton Watson 1973

The Lion's Roar of Queen Śrīmālā, tr. Alex and Hideko Wayman 1974

Courtier and Commoner in Ancient China: Selections from the History of the Former Han by Pan Ku, tr. Burton Watson. Also in paperback ed. 1974

Japanese Literature in Chinese, vol. 1: *Poetry and Prose in Chinese by Japanese Writers of the Early Period*, tr. Burton Watson 1975

Japanese Literature in Chinese, vol. 2: *Poetry and Prose in Chinese by Japanese Writers of the Later Period*, tr. Burton Watson 1976

Love Song of the Dark Lord: Jayadeva's Gītagovinda, tr. Barbara Stoler Miller. Also in paperback ed. Cloth ed. includes critical text of the Sanskrit. 1977; rev. ed. 1997

Ryōkan: Zen Monk-Poet of Japan, tr. Burton Watson 1977
Calming the Mind and Discerning the Real: From the Lam rim chen mo of Tsoṇ-kha-pa, tr. Alex Wayman 1978
The Hermit and the Love-Thief: Sanskrit Poems of Bhartrihari and Bilhaṇa, tr. Barbara Stoler Miller 1978
The Lute: Kao Ming's P'i-p'a chi, tr. Jean Mulligan. Also in paperback ed. 1980
A Chronicle of Gods and Sovereigns: Jinnō Shōtōki of Kitabatake Chikafusa, tr. H. Paul Varley 1980
Among the Flowers: The Hua-chien chi, tr. Lois Fusek 1982
Grass Hill: Poems and Prose by the Japanese Monk Gensei, tr. Burton Watson 1983
Doctors, Diviners, and Magicians of Ancient China: Biographies of Fang-shih, tr. Kenneth J. DeWoskin. Also in paperback ed. 1983
Theater of Memory: The Plays of Kālidāsa, ed. Barbara Stoler Miller. Also in paperback ed. 1984
The Columbia Book of Chinese Poetry: From Early Times to the Thirteenth Century, ed. and tr. Burton Watson. Also in paperback ed. 1984
Poems of Love and War: From the Eight Anthologies and the Ten Long Poems of Classical Tamil, tr. A. K. Ramanujan. Also in paperback ed. 1985
The Bhagavad Gita: Krishna's Counsel in Time of War, tr. Barbara Stoler Miller 1986
The Columbia Book of Later Chinese Poetry, ed. and tr. Jonathan Chaves. Also in paperback ed. 1986
The Tso Chuan: Selections from China's Oldest Narrative History, tr. Burton Watson 1989
Waiting for the Wind: Thirty-Six Poets of Japan's Late Medieval Age, tr. Steven Carter 1989
Selected Writings of Nichiren, ed. Philip B. Yampolsky 1990
Saigyō, Poems of a Mountain Home, tr. Burton Watson 1990
The Book of Lieh Tzu: A Classic of the Tao, tr. A. C. Graham. Morningside ed. 1990
The Tale of an Anklet: An Epic of South India—The Cilappatikāram of Iḷaṇkō Aṭikaḷ, tr. R. Parthasarathy 1993
Waiting for the Dawn: A Plan for the Prince, tr. with introduction by Wm. Theodore de Bary 1993

Yoshitsune and the Thousand Cherry Trees: A Masterpiece of the Eighteenth-Century Japanese Puppet Theater, tr., annotated, and with introduction by Stanleigh H. Jones Jr. 1993

The Lotus Sutra, tr. Burton Watson. Also in paperback ed. 1993

The Classic of Changes: A New Translation of the I Ching as Interpreted by Wang Bi, tr. Richard John Lynn 1994

Beyond Spring: Tz'u Poems of the Sung Dynasty, tr. Julie Landau 1994

The Columbia Anthology of Traditional Chinese Literature, ed. Victor H. Mair 1994

Scenes for Mandarins: The Elite Theater of the Ming, tr. Cyril Birch 1995

Letters of Nichiren, ed. Philip B. Yampolsky; tr. Burton Watson et al. 1996

Unforgotten Dreams: Poems by the Zen Monk Shōtetsu, tr. Steven D. Carter 1997

The Vimalakirti Sutra, tr. Burton Watson 1997

Japanese and Chinese Poems to Sing: The Wakan rōei shū, tr. J. Thomas Rimer and Jonathan Chaves 1997

Breeze Through Bamboo: Kanshi of Ema Saikō, tr. Hiroaki Sato 1998

A Tower for the Summer Heat, by Li Yu, tr. Patrick Hanan 1998

Traditional Japanese Theater: An Anthology of Plays, by Karen Brazell 1998

The Original Analects: Sayings of Confucius and His Successors (0479–0249), by E. Bruce Brooks and A. Taeko Brooks 1998

The Classic of the Way and Virtue: A New Translation of the Tao-te ching of Laozi as Interpreted by Wang Bi, tr. Richard John Lynn 1999

The Four Hundred Songs of War and Wisdom: An Anthology of Poems from Classical Tamil, The Puṛanāṇūṛu, ed. and tr. George L. Hart and Hank Heifetz 1999

Original Tao: Inward Training (Nei-yeh) *and the Foundations of Taoist Mysticism*, by Harold D. Roth 1999

Po Chü-i: Selected Poems, tr. Burton Watson 2000

Lao Tzu's Tao Te Ching: *A Translation of the Startling New Documents Found at Guodian*, by Robert G. Henricks 2000

The Shorter Columbia Anthology of Traditional Chinese Literature, ed. Victor H. Mair 2000

Mistress and Maid (Jiaohongji), by Meng Chengshun, tr. Cyril Birch 2001

Chikamatsu: Five Late Plays, tr. and ed. C. Andrew Gerstle 2001

The Essential Lotus: Selections from the Lotus Sutra, tr. Burton Watson 2002

Early Modern Japanese Literature: An Anthology, 1600–1900, ed. Haruo Shirane 2002; abridged 2008
The Columbia Anthology of Traditional Korean Poetry, ed. Peter H. Lee 2002
The Sound of the Kiss, or The Story That Must Never Be Told: Pingali Suranna's Kalapurnodayamu, tr. Vecheru Narayana Rao and David Shulman 2003
The Selected Poems of Du Fu, tr. Burton Watson 2003
Far Beyond the Field: Haiku by Japanese Women, tr. Makoto Ueda 2003
Just Living: Poems and Prose by the Japanese Monk Tonna, ed. and tr. Steven D. Carter 2003
Han Feizi: Basic Writings, tr. Burton Watson 2003
Mozi: Basic Writings, tr. Burton Watson 2003
Xunzi: Basic Writings, tr. Burton Watson 2003
Zhuangzi: Basic Writings, tr. Burton Watson 2003
The Awakening of Faith, Attributed to Aśvaghosha, tr. Yoshito S. Hakeda, introduction by Ryūichi Abé 2005
The Tales of the Heike, tr. Burton Watson, ed. Haruo Shirane 2006
Tales of Moonlight and Rain, by Ueda Akinari, tr. with introduction by Anthony H. Chambers 2007
Traditional Japanese Literature: An Anthology, Beginnings to 1600, ed. Haruo Shirane 2007
The Philosophy of Qi, by Kaibara Ekken, tr. Mary Evelyn Tucker 2007
The Analects of Confucius, tr. Burton Watson 2007
The Art of War: Sun Zi's Military Methods, tr. Victor Mair 2007
One Hundred Poets, One Poem Each: A Translation of the Ogura Hyakunin Isshu, tr. Peter McMillan 2008
Zeami: Performance Notes, tr. Tom Hare 2008
Zongmi on Chan, tr. Jeffrey Lyle Broughton 2009
Scripture of the Lotus Blossom of the Fine Dharma, rev. ed., tr. Leon Hurvitz, preface and introduction by Stephen R. Teiser 2009
Mencius, tr. Irene Bloom, ed. with an introduction by Philip J. Ivanhoe 2009
Clouds Thick, Whereabouts Unknown: Poems by Zen Monks of China, Charles Egan 2010
The Mozi: A Complete Translation, tr. Ian Johnston 2010
The Huainanzi: A Guide to the Theory and Practice of Government in Early Han China, by Liu An, tr. and ed. John S. Major, Sarah A. Queen, Andrew

Seth Meyer, and Harold D. Roth, with Michael Puett and Judson Murray 2010

The Demon at Agi Bridge and Other Japanese Tales, tr. Burton Watson, ed. with introduction by Haruo Shirane 2011

Haiku Before Haiku: From the Renga Masters to Bashō, tr. with introduction by Steven D. Carter 2011

The Columbia Anthology of Chinese Folk and Popular Literature, ed. Victor H. Mair and Mark Bender 2011

Tamil Love Poetry: The Five Hundred Short Poems of the Aiṅkuṟunūṟu, tr. and ed. Martha Ann Selby 2011

The Teachings of Master Wuzhu: Zen and Religion of No-Religion, by Wendi L. Adamek 2011

The Essential Huainanzi, by Liu An, tr. and ed. John S. Major, Sarah A. Queen, Andrew Seth Meyer, and Harold D. Roth 2012

The Dao of the Military: Liu An's Art of War, tr. Andrew Seth Meyer 2012

Unearthing the Changes: Recently Discovered Manuscripts of the Yi Jing (I Ching) *and Related Texts*, Edward L. Shaughnessy 2013

Record of Miraculous Events in Japan: The Nihon ryōiki, tr. Burton Watson 2013

The Complete Works of Zhuangzi, tr. Burton Watson 2013

Lust, Commerce, and Corruption: An Account of What I Have Seen and Heard, *by an Edo Samurai*, tr. and ed. Mark Teeuwen and Kate Wildman Nakai with Miyazaki Fumiko, Anne Walthall, and John Breen 2014; rev. ed. 2017

Exemplary Women of Early China: The Lienü zhuan *of Liu Xiang*, tr. Anne Behnke Kinney 2014

The Columbia Anthology of Yuan Drama, ed. C. T. Hsia, Wai-yee Li, and George Kao 2014

The Resurrected Skeleton: From Zhuangzi to Lu Xun, by Wilt L. Idema 2014

The Sarashina Diary: *A Woman's Life in Eleventh-Century Japan*, by Sugawara no Takasue no Musume, tr. with introduction by Sonja Arntzen and Itō Moriyuki 2014

The Kojiki: *An Account of Ancient Matters*, by Ō no Yasumaro, tr. Gustav Heldt 2014

The Orphan of Zhao *and Other Yuan Plays: The Earliest Known Versions*, tr. and introduced by Stephen H. West and Wilt L. Idema 2014

www.ingramcontent.com/pod-product-compliance
Ingram Content Group UK Ltd.
Pitfield, Milton Keynes, MK11 3LW, UK
UKHW032040230125
454070UK00004B/168

9 780231 184397